UFO
MYSTERIES

Inexplicable Events and Strange Occurrences

THERE'S SOMETHING STRANGE going on in our world. Consider, if you will, the pulsating, shapeshifting UFO sighted by multiple witnesses near Edinburgh, Scotland, and captured on videotape for over forty minutes. Or the threatening radioactive object that crashed in a frozen pond in New Hampshire, melting the ice and sending the state government into a tailspin. Or the bizarre government misinformation and smear campaign targeted at a prominent UFO researcher.

Journalist and ufologist Curt Sutherly interviewed eyewitnesses and personally investigated many of these remarkable stories. They represent some of the most gripping reports from his thirty years of experience investigating inexplicable events and strange occurrences. These mysteries make us acutely aware of how little we understand our world and the universe beyond. Turn the page—and prepare to come face-to-face with the unknown.

About the Author

Curt Sutherly (Pennsylvania) is a professional journalist with more than thirty years' experience investigating UFOs and paranormal phenomena. His articles have been published in a variety of magazines, including *Strange Magazine* and *Psychic World*. Sutherly is a Vietnam-era veteran of the U.S. Air Force, who is currently employed in the federal civil service.

To Write to the Author

If you wish to contact the author or would like more information about this book, please write to the author in care of Llewellyn Worldwide and we will forward your request. Both the author and publisher appreciate hearing from you and learning of your enjoyment of this book and how it has helped you. Llewellyn Worldwide cannot guarantee that every letter written to the author can be answered, but all will be forwarded. Please write to:

Curt Sutherly
℅ Llewellyn Worldwide
P.O. Box 64383, Dept. 0-7387-0106-8
St. Paul, MN 55164-0383, U.S.A.
Please enclose a self-addressed stamped envelope for reply,
or $1.00 to cover costs. If outside U.S.A., enclose
international postal reply coupon.

Many of Llewellyn's authors have websites with additional information and resources. For more information, please visit our website at:

http://www.llewellyn.com

A Reporter Seeks the Truth

Curt Sutherly

2001
Llewellyn Publications
St. Paul, Minnesota 55164-0383, U.S.A.

First Edition
First Printing, 2001

Book design and editing by Michael Maupin
Cover art © 2001 by Steve Holt
Cover design by Kevin R. Brown
Photos courtesy the R. Hilberg collection except page 109, courtesy U.S. Air Force, and page 128, courtesy NASA.

Library of Congress Cataloging-in-Publication Data
Sutherly, Curt, 1950–
   UFO Mysteries : A reporter seeks the truth / Curt Sutherly.
      p.   cm.
   Includes bibiographical references and index.
   ISBN 0-7387-0106-8
   1. Human-alien encounters. 2. Unidentified flying objects—sightings and encounters.
I. Title: UFO Mysteries. II. Title

BF2050.S87 2001
001.942—dc21   2001038834

"They Don't Know a Damn Thing," "Invasion of Boshkung Lake," "Black Squares and Electric Railroad Lanterns," "The Disinformation Game," "Dark Moons, Red World," and "A Gathering" previously appeared in *Strange Encounters*, Llewellyn Publications, 1996.

Llewellyn Publications
A Division of Llewellyn Worldwide, Ltd.
P.O. Box 64383, Dept. 0-7387-0106-8
St. Paul, MN 55164-0383, U.S.A.
www.llewellyn.com

♻ Printed in the United States of America on recycled paper.

Also by Curt Sutherly

Strange Encounters

This book is for Jim and Paula Rhule:
for abiding friendship
and long, late-night debates.

Acknowledgments

Considering that this is not an entirely new volume—derived, in part, from an earlier work, one would think this book should have been easily and quickly written. Alas, it was not so. The additional necessary research, along with time constraints arising from my full-time job, found me at the task far longer than anticipated.

As with the earlier book, there are many to whom I am indebted. My thanks and appreciation to researchers Ron Halliday and Peter Davenport for the use of key quotations and information. Halliday, who resides in the vicinity of Glasgow, Scotland, is well-known in his homeland as an author, lecturer, and UFO investigator. Davenport is head of the National UFO Reporting Center in Seattle, and provides an indispensable service to police, civilian investigators, and members of the news media.

Another who provides an indispensable service is longtime researcher Lucius Farish. Nearly the entire second appendix of this book as well as information scattered throughout exist only because of Lou's *UFO Newsclipping Service* (No. 2 Caney Valley Drive, Plumerville, Arkansas 72127). His is undoubtedly the best regular compilation of its sort available anywhere.

I would also like to thank Rick Hilberg, who not only provided information and inspiration via phone and mail from his home in Cleveland, but also managed to keep me from perpetuating at least one significant historical error committed by previous writers.

John A. Keel is another to whom I own special thanks.

John was my mentor when, as a young man, I plunged headlong into the murky realm of ufology. The lessons he taught were based on his own considerable experience as a journalist and investigator, and they have not been forgotten.

Likewise, I must thank James W. Moseley for his insight, wit, and inspiration. I've known Jim for many years and have come to respect his accumulated knowledge, wisdom, and—*yes!*—even his cynicism.

Others to whom I am indebted include Robert C. Warth, who for many years published *Pursuit*, and who has graciously granted the use of material from that august journal; James Oberg, space engineer, author, and international space expert, for use of included material; Denise Voshell, for jogging my memory of certain events and individuals; Lisa Christopher, at the Carlisle Camera Shop, for her help and expertise; and to Larry Zeigler, Elmer B. Weaver, David Fideler, Robert J. Durant, Eugene Steinberg, Carol Hilberg, Loren Coleman, Jerome Clark, Allen H. Greenfield, Stanton T. Friedman, Dr. Charles L. Wiedemann, Stan Gordon, Betty Hill, Philip J. Klass, John R. Lindermuth, Kevin D. Randle, Brad Steiger, Geneva Hagen, Ronald L. Kaylor, Floyd Murray, Robert S. Easley, and everyone at Llewellyn who worked on this project, particularly Nancy Mostad and Ann Kerns in Acquisitions, Kevin Brown and Lynne Menturweck in the Art department, and my editor this time around, Michael Maupin.

C. K. S.

CONTENTS

The man is wisest who, like Socrates,
knows that his wisdom is worth nothing.

THESE WORDS WERE written by the Greek philosopher Plato, and since his death in the year 347 B.C., the sum of human knowledge has grown immeasurably. And yet, Plato's words remain true. Our wisdom, our knowledge, is nothing. Smart as we think we are, arrogant as we often are, we remain surrounded by the unknown and thwarted by the unknowable.

I've spent a fair amount of time in pursuit of the unknown— investigating various phenomena that defy conventional wisdom or explanation. Sometimes I've felt very near to an understanding of some particular strange event or occurrence. But at other times I've felt like an imbecile; I've felt as though I knew nothing at all.

The only son and the oldest (by several years) of four siblings, I grew up a voracious reader. One of the books I read at an early age was an inexpensive paperback titled *The Book of the Damned*. The author was a man named Charles Hoy Fort, and in the opening lines he explained his title. He said, "By the damned, I mean the excluded. We shall have a procession of data that Science has excluded."

Fort explored such diverse mysteries as eerie lights and strange aerial objects, black rains and lake monsters, lost planets and strange ancient artifacts, to mention a very few. And throughout it all, he attacked science for insisting on ignoring these mysteries. "Dogmatic Science," he called it. Eventually he wrote three other titles dealing with strange phenomena: *Lo!*, *New Lands*, and *Wild Talents* (the last published shortly after his death). Fort wrote with humor and acid wit, and was something of a philosopher besides. Plato and Fort probably would have gotten on famously, had they lived in the same era.

Fort died on May 3, 1932, at the age of fifty-seven. He died unappreciated and, I suspect, lonely, in part because of his insistence on attacking scientific dogma. But what he lacked in life was gained in death; appreciation and audience came to him posthumously. His books have been devoured by generations of readers recognizing the challenge of his words.

Fort's philosophy was to accept nothing, question everything. He would say, if alive today, "Look carefully at the world around you and re-examine what you think you know."

★ ★ ★

Without a doubt, Fort influenced my early thinking. I read everything I could find on "fortean" phenomena, and continued doing so for several years. There came a time, however, when one particular fortean subject fascinated me more than the rest: the subject of unidentified flying objects or UFOs. By the late 1960s this interest had grown measurably, coinciding with my enlistment in the United States Air Force. This was also around the time I discovered the writings of John A. Keel.

A veteran journalist, John had trekked through the Orient in the 1950s, sleuthing out the mystery and magic of faraway lands. His cliffhanging experiences resulted in a book, *Jadoo*, published in 1957. Back in the states in the 1960s, he began a long-term investigation of the UFO phenomenon. (He once said, "I thought

I was smart enough to figure it all out.") Several books and count-less articles resulted, and in each John made it abundantly clear that he doubted the conventional wisdom (among those who believed at all) that UFOs were alien spacecraft.

In 1972, John and I met in Washington, D.C., where he was working as a consultant for the Department of Health, Education, and Welfare. At the time I was beginning to entertain doubts of my own that UFOs were extraterrestrial spacecraft; but the UFO issue was only part of the reason I wanted to meet Keel. Truth is, I admired him. He was a genuine "Indiana Jones" long before the creation of the cinematic hero; and his skill as a writer, his wit, and narrative ability were standards by which I determined to measure my own early writing.

I was honorably discharged from the military in September 1972. In November of that year my first freelance story appeared, published in a daily newspaper. The story was a travel piece, but it also contained a warning about the consequences of overpopu-lation as well as elements of fortean mystery. On the heels of this small personal triumph came disaster: a car accident landed me in a hospital in early December. A team of surgeons reconstructed my right cheekbone and right eye socket. A loop of reinforcing alloy wire is still embedded in my cheek.

For a time I worked odd jobs while simultaneously moving deeper into the study of UFOs. I investigated dozens of reported sightings, interviewed countless witnesses, and wrote about all of it. I was also, by then, spending weekends at the New Jersey farm of the late Ivan T. Sanderson.

A zoologist and writer, Ivan was founder of the Society for the Investigation of the Unexplained (SITU), then headquartered at his farm. He had traveled widely in his life, seeking out new plant and animal species for exhibition in zoos and botanical gardens. He had also written a good many books, mostly about wildlife and the natural sciences; but others dealt with fortean matters, includ-ing UFOs.

As a zoologist, Ivan became interested in the early reports of a hairy, manlike giant said to be living in the Himalayan mountains—the so-called Abominable Snowman. This interest led to his 1961 book, *Abominable Snowman: Legend Come to Life*. Ivan was curious about many things and that curiosity, along with a suggestion by the cryptozoologist Loren Coleman, resulted in the eventual formation of SITU. Because the society was headquartered at the Sanderson farm, many of Ivan's zoological buddies inevitably found themselves assisting, one way or another, in its operation.

In 1972, I was making my first trip to the farm, the last mile or so of which followed an unmarked, unpaved, country road with many diverging paths. I'd been forewarned during a phone conversation that I would never find the place without an escort, and was told that someone from the society would meet me at a particular location. I arrived a bit early, but soon a station wagon drove up bearing SITU markings. An enormous, powerful man got out of the car. He approached, grinned, and stuck out his hand, which engulfed my own: "My name is Ryhiner," he said, shaking me up and down. "Pete Ryhiner. If you have trouble recalling that, just think of rhinoceros."

Ryhiner was a professional animal collector and a longtime friend and associate of Ivan's. He was also, as I found out, a gourmet cook schooled in Switzerland. That night he prepared a veritable feast attended by Ivan and Alma Sanderson, myself, and several of Ivan's friends. During dinner, Ivan regaled us with stories of his misspent youth and of his years exploring jungles and rain forests around the world. Afterward, I was recruited to assist in scrubbing the pots and pans literally blackened by Ryhiner while cooking.

While these stories are amusing to recall, what I remember most about my visits to Ivan's farm were the discussions he and I had about writing. Ivan was one of two writers I have known who could produce a lengthy, printable story first draft, no revisions. (John R. Lindermuth, a former newspaper colleague, was the other.) Ivan wrote on an old manual typewriter with a continuous roll of paper fixed over the machine. When the story or book was completed, he would cut the roll into pages and submit them to his publisher. He wrote in the same way he spoke—an easy, often folksy speech that anyone could follow and enjoy. During our conversations he encouraged me to maximize my own potential as a writer, even though at the time I was barely a novice.

I vividly recall the night Ivan asked me to become the resident caretaker of his farm. In exchange, he offered to serve as my mentor in matters of writing as well as in the natural sciences and other disciplines at his command. When I later declined, Alma, dying of cancer, urged me to reconsider. She did so in private, without consulting Ivan, and I'll never forget the pain in her eyes. Being a foolish young man, I failed to accept even then.

Following Alma's death, Ivan remarried. On February 19, 1973, at sixty-two, he too succumbed to cancer. With his death, others took the reins of the society, among them Robert C. Warth, Steven Mayne, and Marty Wiegler. For a brief time, John Keel served as editor-in-chief of *Pursuit*, SITU's journal. He in turn appointed me senior writer—a circumstance that lasted about a year.

With the new pecking order established, Keel took off for Scandinavia to gather information on a long-running and widespread UFO flap. At about the same time a new and talented researcher came along. Out of respect for the man and the friendship we shared, I'll not use his true name. Instead, I'll call him Raymond.

★　★　★

Like many others, Raymond had a strong interest in the UFO phenomenon. He was a consummate writer, his talent evident in articles published in *Pursuit*, *Fate*, and similar journals. His instincts were sharp and his mind extremely quick. Within a few months he made a transition that had taken others years to make if they made it at all: he dismissed the prevailing belief that UFOs are extraterrestrial spacecraft and began working under the assumption that something far more odd and complex is at work. But his sharp mind and intuitive grasp were also his undoing.

Immersed as we were in the study of UFOs, many of us at the time failed to recognize the potential for emotional or psychological harm arising from such studies. For Raymond and a number of others, myself included, the unrelenting (and often undisciplined) pursuit of the UFO mystery was worsened by a belief that the phenomenon was more metaphysical than physical. To accept, on our terms, the occurrence of UFOs was to accept the notion that all of reality originates on a mental or metaphysical plane, and is limited only by our subconscious beliefs.

In any event, we became obsessed with this view. At the same time, bizarre occurrences became almost commonplace. For Raymond, it became a nightmare.

The man spent more and more time absorbed in trying to prove our "solution" to the UFO puzzle. From all outward signs this resulted in problems in his home. (He was married and had a beautiful family.) His stress level soared and small wonder: UFOs and strange creatures were suddenly everywhere within driving distance of his house. In the creature department, hairy man-beasts and even lizardmen were reported. Mysterious screams and sounds issued from area forests. Nocturnal lights in the sky (and on the ground) were spotted routinely. Unusual deaths of animals began to occur, serving to intensify the already rampant fear and paranoia. (In one of the worst of these episodes, a farmer's rabbits were removed from their pens and killed. Some were torn apart. Others were crushed as if by huge, powerful hands; the broken bodies were left lying atop the pens.)

In my rented cottage some two hundred miles away, the telephone became an instrument of great annoyance. My conversations were routinely interrupted by strange sounds and third-party voices. Important files began to disappear. For example, I'd finish drafting a magazine article on my old manual typewriter and place it in a file-folder for later editing. On retrieving the file, I'd find the folder inexplicably empty.

Outside the cottage, my car developed a talent for turning on its own headlights. In one instance, I drove to a nearby village to purchase groceries and to check with the post office about a parcel delivery. While in the grocery store talking with the owner's son, my car lights switched on. It was midday and the car was in full view from the front window of the store. I returned to the vehicle and switched off the lights, then drove to the post office where I carefully checked the light switch before leaving the car. When I returned, the lights were back on. I switched them off a second time and drove home, feeling exasperated. Inside the cottage, the telephone began to ring. When I answered, there was no response, only a metallic echo. As I cursed the phone, I looked out the window at my parked car. The headlights were back on.

Raymond's own difficulty, meanwhile, was compounded by his fear for his family. He expressed this in one of the last letters I received from him. He said, "You and I know that most (or all) of these phenomena do indeed originate in the unconscious mind. I am beginning to worry about what might happen in or around my own home. I know of no way to shake such 'thoughts' from my unconscious mind, of course, so I feel frustrated in my desire to stop the events short of my property line."

His fears were realized soon after, when huge, three-toed creature tracks were founds outside his home. I recall sitting in Raymond's living room while he went to another room to retrieve a cast of one of the tracks. The cast was enormous and quite deep, and sent shivers down my spine. The "animal" that made it would have had to weigh one thousand pounds or more.

Not long after, I received the final letter. In it, Raymond severed all ties, expressing a desire for no further contact. I recognized in his words the panic and dismay of an embattled man. Others, too, received the letter, or one similar. Several months later I also withdrew from the field.

I was, by then, a full-time newspaper reporter, anxious to develop my skills. In addition, I was uneasy over Raymond's departure and I sensed a growing unhappiness among other formerly enthusiastic researchers. So I bowed out and went on to write "general assignment" stories about local government, crime, and community events, and finally, to create a weekly outdoor column.

* * *

For ten years I stayed away from fortean phenomena. I became a jock. Under the tutelage of my friend and athletic mentor, Randy Brandt, I trained as a sprinter and long-distance runner, and competed successfully in adult track and field events. I traveled extensively during this period. In Puerto Rico, I explored old San Juan and entered majestic El Yunque, the rain forest. In the desert Southwest, I climbed through ancient ruins and walked modern cities. In the remote forests of northern Quebec, I watched the delighted smile of a Cree Indian boy at his first taste of spiced sausage.

I fell in love. I married and divorced, and found my life in ruin. I paid a visit to Hell. When I returned, I dusted off my old leather jacket and again changed my career. Then I received a phone call. Over the ensuing months a series of freelance articles followed, the first I'd written on any fortean subject in a decade—which brings me to the present and the book you hold.

The chapters that make up this volume (and a second to eventually follow, both based on an earlier mass market edition) are culled from years of files, interviews and experience. I have gone to some effort to verify and document sources while at the same time trying to create a book that is both entertaining and more personal than its antecedent—a book to be used and enjoyed by anyone interested in the subject, not just by a small group of knowledgeable UFO enthusiasts.

One other thing I have done in this volume that I did not do in the original: I have offered a conclusion.

Curt Sutherly
Indiantown Gap, Pennsylvania
December 1999

part one

1947 to 1975:
The Era Begins

The UFO phenomenon exists on the borderline between reality . . . and imagination.

Allen H. Greenfield

CHAPTER 1

"They Don't Know a Damn Thing..."

THROUGHOUT THE WORLD, 1947 was a spectacular year in aviation. New records and standards for flight were established, and just as quickly broken.

At Muroc Field (now Edwards AFB) in California, a group of Air Force aviators and technicians pursued an "impossible" goal and succeeded—they broke the sound barrier. One of their number was a war ace named Chuck Yeager, who was also a gifted test pilot. The craft was a small orange rocket plane designed by Bell Aircraft: the X-1.

The air-launched X-1 was hauled aloft by a B-29 bomber. At twenty thousand feet, the machine and pilot were dropped and the rockets ignited. The first test flight was conducted in December 1946. The pilot was a civilian, Chalmers "Slick" Goodlin. But it was Yeager at the controls on October 14, 1947—the day the barrier fell. Forty years later, he related in his book *Press On* that what was most remarkable about the flight "was what didn't happen.

3

We didn't disintegrate didn't 'hit the wall,' didn't even feel a bump when we went supersonic."[1]

Thanks to military secrecy, nine months would pass before the outside world knew of Yeager's accomplishment.

While all this was going on the Northrop Corporation was completing development of a "flying wing" for the fledgling United States Air Force.[2] An early prototype, the XB-35, flew in June 1946, and a jet version, the YB-49, flew the following year. The YB-49 crashed in 1948 while being tested by Capt. Glenn Edwards (Muroc Field was renamed in his honor). A second B-49 burned during a taxiing accident, and a third was scrapped. A number of others were ordered destroyed on the assembly line. Years later, before his death, John K. Northrop claimed the flying wing program was deliberately canceled by the secretary of the Air Force, Stuart Symington, for political reasons and not for technical problems as was reported at the time.[3]

While the Air Force was still testing the flying wing, the United States Navy was working on its own version: a prop-driven, circular machine, the XF5U-1, otherwise known as the "flying flapjack." The aircraft was designed to ascend vertically and hover as well as fly horizontally. The test program was carried out at Muroc Field under security so tight even the Air Force was kept in the dark. But in the end the Navy's flapjack went the way of the Northrop wing, pushed aside in favor of more conventional jet-powered aircraft.

Elsewhere, on California's Long Beach Harbor on November 2, millionaire aircraft designer Howard Hughes piloted a machine many said would never fly: the world's largest flying boat, known affectionately as the "Spruce Goose." With a 320-foot wingspan and measuring 219 feet, the 190-ton Goose raised seventy feet during a one-thousand-yard test run. Afterward, Hughes thumbed his nose at a skeptical world and hangared the aircraft, while he never again flew.[4]

The following month, on December 10, aviatrix Jacqueline Cochran piloted her P-51 Mustang over a measured one-hundred-

Kenneth Arnold (center)—the first pilot to officially report unidentified flying objects—is flanked in this early photo by United Airlines pilot Captain E. J. Smith (left) and co-pilot Ralph E. Stevens. On July 4, 1947, Smith and Stevens spotted nine disc-shaped objects just after their aircraft departed the Boise, Idaho, airport. Smith later joined Arnold during a UFO investigation in Tacoma, Washington.

kilometer course at an average speed of nearly 470 miles per hour, establishing a new record. She added to her achievement the following year, setting a record pace over a one-thousand-kilometer course at an average speed of 431 miles per hour.

Throughout this period the changes in aircraft design were incessant and ongoing—a result of rigorous testing of new airframes mated to postwar jet engine technology.

Enter a flier named Kenneth Arnold. Like others during this period, he made it into the record books. His is listed in *Air Facts and Feats: A Record of International Aerospace Achievement.*[5] But unlike all the others, Arnold was not a test pilot or a stunt flier.

A twenty-eight-year-old private pilot and owner of a fire-control equipment company in Boise, Idaho, Arnold was aloft in his single-engine plane on the afternoon of June 24, 1947, assisting in a search for a crashed C-46 Marine transport. The day was sunny and clear—a beautiful day, he would later recall.

The veteran pilot had departed Chehalis (Washington) Airport at about 2:00 P.M., and was in the vicinity of Mount Rainier an hour later when he was surprised by a flash that reflected from the side of his airplane. When a second flash occurred, Arnold located the source: nine objects gleaming in the sun as they flew south from the direction of Mount Baker, flying in echelon formation, sweeping back and forth among the peaks.

Amazed, Arnold nonetheless had enough presence of mind to triangulate the speed of the objects as they passed between Rainier and Mount Adams, forty-five miles to the south. His computations suggested the impossible: the objects were traveling at about sixteen hundred miles per hour, far faster than any known aircraft—much faster even than the secret Bell X-1 which, in exceeding Mach 1 later in the year, would travel at seven hundred miles per hour. (The speed of sound is 660 miles per hour at forty thousand feet.)

Arnold described the motion of the objects as unusual, like "speedboats on rough water," or "like a saucer . . . if you skipped it across water." The sighting thrust him into the spotlight. Unwillingly, he became a celebrity—the first pilot to officially report and document the sighting of UFOs.

★ ★ ★

Although not one to seek publicity, Arnold felt he needed to report his sighting. He had a sudden fear that the strange silvery objects might be experimental aircraft flown by the Soviet Union, America's newest archenemy. Landing at the Yakima, Washington, airport, he told his story to several curious listeners. The following morning he flew to Pendleton, Oregon, where skeptical reporters awaited him. He subsequently spoke with Bill Bequette, a reporter for the Pendleton *East Oregonian.*

After hearing Arnold's account, Bequette wrote a four-paragraph story in which he incorrectly reported that Arnold was a member of the Boise "fire control." This subsequently resulted in Arnold being mistakenly identified as a U.S. Forest Service employee. Bequette dispatched his story to the Associated Press and went to lunch. When he returned, he learned that reporters from all over the country had been telephoning for more information. He dispatched a longer story that afternoon and the craziness grew worse.

A week later, on July 8, 1947, the Army Air Force announced that a crashed flying disc had been retrieved in New Mexico. Almost immediately, Army higher headquarters recanted the story. For a time, government and public officials regarded the rash of "flying saucer" reports as a form of postwar hysteria. They decided it would eventually fade, but it never did. Today the sightings continue, with many reports made by sane, sober people whose testimony would be acceptable in a court of law, but who nonetheless remain open to public harassment and media ridicule.

It was no different for Ken Arnold. He was plagued by individuals who hounded him for details, and by news reporters who were all too anxious to put their particular spin to his story.

As a journalist, I had the distinction of being one of the last persons to ever interview Ken Arnold. As such it wasn't much of an interview, conducted briefly and by telephone. But it was substantially more than anyone had gotten from the man in a long time.

The interview was conducted on June 24, 1976, the anniversary of Arnold's sighting.[6] At the time, I was in touch with UFO and fortean researchers throughout the country while earning a meager living as a writer of magazine articles and occasional newspaper copy. Most of the time I was broke and the money I received from sales of stories, when it arrived (the checks were almost always overdue), was used to finance the pursuit of new mysteries in new locations. Because I was young, travel and adventure seemed more important than regular meals and a roof over my head.

At some point during all of this I obtained a copy of a book called *The Coming of the Saucers*, co-written by Ken Arnold and publisher Ray Palmer. The story, told in a simple, straightforward narrative, recounted Arnold's experiences in the weeks after his Mount Rainier sighting. It was a hair-raising account—an adventure straight out of pulp fiction. I was fascinated, but also suspicious: Palmer had been a publisher of science fiction, so how much of the book was fact and how much was fiction?

I began to inquire around, trying to determine the whereabouts of Ken Arnold. But my various contacts were unable to help. "Isn't Arnold dead?" someone suggested. Another said he had heard that Arnold and family had moved to Australia to escape the constant harassment from reporters and UFO enthusiasts. The truth, as I discovered, was far simpler: the man was still living in Idaho. I located him by phoning long-distance and asking for directory assistance.

When I identified myself, Arnold replied, "I'm pretty fed up with reporters." He said that people from his regional paper, the *Idaho Daily Statesman*, had been seeking an interview for years. In one instance when a reporter telephoned: "I listened to his reasons and then I quietly hung up."

Afraid of exactly that response, I eased into the conversation. I said that I was not only a writer but also an aviation enthusiast (which was true, I'd worked as an aircraft crew chief in the Air Force), so for a few minutes we talked aviation before drifting back to the original subject. In the process, I must have conveyed some small knowledge of the UFO phenomenon, for Arnold said abruptly: "You seem to understand this [UFO] business pretty well; did you by chance read my book? Most reporters have never even looked at it, which is part of the reason I won't talk to them. They don't know a damn thing other than that I saw flying saucers."

At this point I explained that I had in fact read his book, and that I was familiar with the essential details but would be only too happy to hear more.

"Well, if you've read the book, you have most of the details," Arnold replied. "You know, the quotes in the book are not made up like a lot of people believe. At the time I owned one of the very early [tape] recorders, and I carried it with me to Tacoma."

* * *

Ken Arnold's sighting near Mount Rainier not only made him an inviting target for the press but also caused him to be inundated with mail. There were so many letters, he said, that "I just couldn't answer them all."

The experience, meanwhile, had prompted him to file a report with the commanding officer at Wright Field, Dayton, Ohio (today Wright Patterson AFB). Also, at about this time, Ray Palmer contacted Arnold and asked the aviator to consider writing a magazine article about his Mount Rainier sighting. Arnold declined to write the article, instead sending Palmer a copy of his report to the Air Force.

A few days later Palmer wrote back, telling Arnold about a letter he had received from a harbor patrol officer near Tacoma, Washington. According to Palmer, the writer of the letter claimed that he and another man had spotted flying discs over Maury Island, a small peninsula located about three miles north of Tacoma Harbor in Puget Sound. The writer further claimed that one of the discs had dropped metallic fragments onto the island. Palmer wanted Arnold to fly to Tacoma and investigate the story, all expenses paid.

Shortly thereafter, Lieutenant Frank Brown and Captain William Davidson, representatives of A-2 Military Intelligence of the Fourth Army Air Force, paid a visit with Arnold. They had been assigned the task of investigating the UFO phenomenon. They questioned Arnold on all aspects of his sighting and then, with the pilot's permission, examined his mail. At the end of their visit the two officers left a telephone number so Arnold could contact them if the need arose.

Several days later, Arnold decided to accept Palmer's offer to investigate the Maury Island incident. He taxied his aircraft to the end of a pasture near his home and throttled forward into what he later called "the doggonest mystery a man could ever dream of."

On the evening of July 29, 1947, he landed at Berry Field, a small airstrip just outside Tacoma where he felt sure no one would recognize him (his picture had been splashed all over the newspapers). When he tried to make hotel reservations via the airfield's telephone, he discovered that every facility was booked and the city was in the throes of a housing shortage.

In a last and seemingly futile attempt to find a place to stay, he telephoned the Winthrop Hotel, the largest and most expensive in the city. He was shocked to learn that a room had been reserved in his name! Only two people knew that Arnold was planning a trip to Tacoma: his wife and Ray Palmer. Neither of them had reserved the room. In fact, Arnold had not even bothered to file a flight plan. He felt certain the hotel clerk was confusing him with another Ken Arnold, but he decided to accept the room, feeling equally certain he'd never find another anywhere in the city.

After settling into the hotel, Arnold checked the local telephone directory and found a listing for Harold Dahl, one of the two harbor patrolmen identified by Ray Palmer. On phoning Dahl, the pilot discovered that the man was reluctant to discuss his sighting. In fact, Dahl rather pointedly told Arnold to forget the matter and go home, but Arnold was persistent and finally convinced the man to stop by the hotel room for an interview. Dahl showed up that same evening, and after a bit of prodding, told his story.

On the afternoon of June 21, 1947, Dahl said he had been operating his boat off Maury Island, accompanied by his son, two crewmen, and the family dog. Suddenly he spotted six "doughnut-shaped" objects flying overhead at an altitude of about two thousand feet. One of the objects appeared to be in trouble as it was gradually losing altitude. It began discharging lava-like material from its underside—material that fell in large quantities on both the boat and the beach at Maury Island. A fragment, Dahl said, hit his son, causing injury to the boy's arm. Another struck and killed his dog. The boat itself was substantially damaged. Following this, all six discs gained altitude and moved off toward the open sea.

According to Dahl, about twenty tons of hot, slag-like material had been dumped onto the beach. After the substance cooled somewhat, the men collected a large quantity of samples and returned to the mainland, where Dahl's boy was hospitalized.

The incident was related to Dahl's superior, Fred Lee Crisman, who at first didn't believe the story, Dahl said. It was Crisman, however, who had sent the letter to Ray Palmer.

The next morning, June 22, a man wearing a black suit and driving a 1947 Buick reportedly visited Dahl. The stranger invited Dahl downtown for breakfast. Dahl accepted, thinking the man was a customer for his part-time salvage operation. Inside a cafe, Dahl said the stranger related the entire sequence of events occurring off Maury Island. He claimed the stranger also told him that it would not be wise to discuss the incident if he wished his family to remain healthy. Strangely, Dahl failed to heed the advice, claiming he immediately drove to the docks where he told fellow workers of this latest episode.

★ ★ ★

On the morning after his interview with Dahl, Arnold received a visit from both Dahl and Fred Crisman. Crisman related what he knew of Dahl's story, adding that when he first heard the tale he was convinced the man was lying to explain away the damage to the boat. However, he said he finally visited Maury Island where he not only found the slag material but also saw one of the doughnut discs cruising overhead.

When Dahl and Crisman departed, Arnold telephoned Captain E. J. Smith, a United Airlines pilot who had also spotted UFOs.[7] Arnold was beginning to suspect he was out of his depth with the investigation and he said as much to Smith. He asked for help. The airline pilot agreed, and Arnold subsequently flew to Seattle to rendezvous with his friend. From then on, events got even stranger.

Every conversation in Arnold's room was monitored by an unseen agency and telephoned verbatim to reporters in the city. The pilots learned of the leak from Ted Morillo, a United Press reporter, who said a mystery informant was phoning in their conversations. The men tore the hotel room apart looking for bugging devices, but found none.

At first, Arnold denied the accuracy of the leaked information. Later, however, he admitted to Morillo that the details were on target. Along with Smith, he began to suspect that either Crisman or Dahl was the source of the leak. But the pilots soon discovered that the phone calls were being made even while the harbor patrolmen were with them in the room. Finally, in desperation, Arnold telephoned the two Army intelligence officers, Lieutenant Brown and Captain Davidson. They arrived the same day, listened to Crisman's recollection of both his and Dahl's alleged sightings, and then suddenly decided they had to leave. (Dahl was not present. He fled the room when he learned the military was being called in.)

"We practically begged them [the Army officers] to stay," Arnold observed during the interview. "But they claimed they had to get their plane to some air show the next day."

The officers departed, carrying slag samples given to them by Crisman. That same night the military plane transporting Brown and Davidson crashed, killing both men. The flight chief and one other person aboard, an Army enlisted man, parachuted to safety.

On the morning of August 1, 1947, the story of the crashed transport appeared in banner headlines in the *Tacoma Times*. The story revealed the names of the two Army officers even before the military officially identified them! The story was by a *Times* staff writer, Paul Lance. His source of information, he later told Arnold and Smith, was the anonymous telephone caller.

Two weeks after the story broke, Paul Lance died unexpectedly. "Maybe it was coincidence," Arnold said.

Ted Morillo, the United Press reporter, subsequently lost his job and suffered numerous personal difficulties. A persistent newsman, he had employed his own network of informants in an effort to trace the identity of the mystery caller. He never succeeded. He finally suggested to Smith and Arnold that they leave town for their own safety.

Crisman disappeared and it was rumored (by the anonymous caller again) that he had departed Tacoma aboard an Alaska-bound military transport. Dahl was found sitting in a movie theater, and according to Arnold seemed unconcerned about the deaths of the two Army intelligence men.

Arnold himself nearly suffered a fate similar to that of the two Army officers. En route home he stopped for fuel. On takeoff, the aircraft engine stalled, and only quick thinking and skilled piloting saved him from a fatal crash.

★　★　★

Following the incident at Tacoma, Ken Arnold grew resentful and angry over what he believed was an inappropriate response to UFO sightings on the part of the government. He said a sense of national loyalty had prompted him to file a report on the strange flying objects, but instead of being congratulated, he, Smith, and other pilots were all "made to look like goddamn jerks."

Arnold and Smith both continued to fly in the years afterward, Smith commercially and Arnold as a private flier. Of his friend Smith, Arnold said, "He retired after thirty-eight years at the age of sixty. They had a banquet in his honor but I couldn't attend."

In 1949 or 1950, Arnold turned down a fifty-thousand-dollar offer from Doubleday for the rights to his story—a tremendous sum from any publisher at the time. "They wanted to have someone ghostwrite the book," Arnold said. "I wanted it in my own words, so I turned down their offer." Film rights too remained with Arnold due to the flier's insistence that the story be documented accurately. In the end, the only complete account of the incident came from Arnold's collaboration with Ray Palmer, first as an article in FATE magazine, and later as the book The Coming of the Saucers. There was, however, another written account—one never intended for public consumption.

Publisher Ray Palmer, at his home in Amherst, Wisconsin, in 1965. In July 1947, Palmer contacted aviator Kenneth Arnold and hired him to fly to Tacoma, Washington, to investigate a reported UFO event. The two men later co-authored a book, *The Coming of the Saucers*, which recounted the strange occurrences in Tacoma. (Photo by Rick Hilberg)

Amid rumors of sabotage and espionage in connection with the crash of the military transport, the FBI initiated a field investigation that included interviews with the various Maury Island players. The result was a fifteen-page report to the director, compiled by Jack B. Wilcox, special agent in charge, in Seattle. The report was dated August 18, 1947.

A copy of the report, made available some years ago under the Freedom of Information Act, remained heavily censored particularly in the matter of names. However, because the chief players were already known through Arnold's account and subsequent stories, it was a simple matter to fit an appropriate name to most blanks.

Judging by the report, the FBI quickly concluded that the Maury Island episode was a hoax. One section of the report, for instance, describes a news interview with Harold Dahl at the subject's home. According to the account, the reporter was attempting to confirm a story about a "disintegrated" disc near Maury Island. However, during the interview, Dahl's wife reportedly went into a "considerable rage" and demanded that her husband admit the story was a fantasy. The interviewer said Dahl then recanted, acknowledging the flying disc story was a hoax.

During an interview with Dahl and Crisman on August 7, 1947, at the bureau office in Tacoma, the resident FBI agent found the two to be vague and evasive in response to questions. The agent said both men initially "denied making any statement to anyone" suggesting that the slag samples came from a flying disc. It was apparent, the agent continued, that the two men "were not telling their complete and true connection with the flying disc story. They refused to give any definite information . . . but gave evasive answers and repeatedly stated that they had nothing to do with it. . . ."

Faced with a lengthy interrogation, Crisman and Dahl finally told the FBI agent that, in communicating with Ray Palmer, they had manufactured a portion of the flying disc story only because it appeared that "that's what he [Palmer] wanted them to say." The FBI interviewer, however, remained unimpressed with what seemed a total and deliberate fabrication, and in his summary reiterated that "no definite information could be obtained . . . as to what each [man] specifically had done to start the flying disc story."

Regarding the crashed military transport (actually a B-25 bomber), the FBI checked with Fourth Army Air Force investigators at McChord Field, Washington. The bureau was told that an Army investigation had uncovered no hint of sabotage linked to the crash. The cause of the crash was reportedly traced to a faulty exhaust stack that sparked a fire on the left wing. The wing sheared away and in the process tore off the aircraft tail. Rumors (spread by the anonymous caller) that the crash was caused by a bomb or by enemy aircraft gunfire were determined to be as false as the flying discs over Maury Island.

(A point here concerns the sudden departure of the Army investigators following their interview with Fred Crisman. The two, Brown and Davidson, must have observed some detail in Crisman's story that gave away the hoax. If so, none of this was conveyed to Arnold, probably because the two officers were under orders to remain silent about anything they discovered.)

Murkier was the identity of the anonymous caller who, among other things, tipped reporters to the identities of Brown and Davidson even before the Army had released the names of the two men. Five anonymous calls were made to various newspaper officers between 11:30 A.M. on July 31, and 5:30 P.M. on August 2, 1947. The FBI clearly suspected Crisman of being responsible for the calls in some way. Even so, the bureau never succeeded in tracing the identity of the caller.[8]

The "fragments" from Maury Island were another matter entirely. Bureau investigators quickly found that they bore a "distinct resemblance" to slag from a smelter near Tacoma. What's more, there is nothing in the FBI report to suggest that the slag was radioactive—something mentioned by others who have attempted to review this episode.

Once it became apparent that the flying disc story was a sham and (at least officially) that the crash of the Army aircraft was an accident and not sabotage, the FBI closed its files on Maury Island.

* * *

Some notes on the principal players:

Fred Crisman never went to Alaska despite rumors to that effect. Instead, according to journalist John Keel,[9] he was caught up in the war in Korea and later became a public school teacher. Crisman eventually adopted the identity of Jon Gold, a radio talk show host in Tacoma. In 1968, District Attorney Jim Garrison, conducting an inquiry into the John Kennedy assassination, summoned Crisman to New Orleans. Crisman was tenuously linked to the assassination through photos taken at the time in Dallas—one of which showed a man who looked like Crisman.

Keel reported that someone tried to kill Crisman just before his summons to New Orleans. The attempt had nothing to do with the death of Kennedy and much to do with Crisman's abrasive radio presence; he had, evidently, antagonized a good many people with his wit and aggressive personality.

Crisman died of natural causes in 1975, leaving ufologists and Kennedy conspiracy theorists to continue to puzzle over the man's past. Many felt he had ties to the intelligence community, particularly the CIA, although the reasoning behind this is as tenuous as his supposed presence in Dallas. On the other hand, Crisman's ability to confound the FBI in Tacoma in 1947, plus his possible connection to the anonymous telephone caller, leaves one to wonder if there isn't some truth in this view.

Soon after the incident Crisman's cohort, Harold Dahl, moved to a different address. Meanwhile, Dahl's teenage son disappeared, only to turn up in another state, reportedly suffering from amnesia. Others have written that authorities found young Dahl in Colorado or Wyoming. According to the FBI, the boy turned up in Montana. There was no mention that the youth suffered from amnesia, simply that he had run away.

Dahl, incidentally, was not and had never been a harbor patrol officer. This was a persona he and Crisman adopted for the sake of their story, although the two did own and operate a supply boat in Tacoma harbor.

Publisher Ray Palmer, who was clearly duped by Crisman into pursuing the Maury Island story, spent his final years in relative obscurity. His death in 1977 brought an end to an era in UFO reporting—silencing what was once perhaps the strongest voice in the field.

Kenneth Arnold lived on for many active years before his death on January 16, 1984, in a hospital in Bellevue, Washington. The fiftieth anniversary of his sighting passed on June 24, 1997 with minimal fanfare, which is probably the way Arnold would have wanted it. Despite his Mount Rainier sighting and his unwanted fame, he never thought of himself as anyone special—maintaining all along that he was "just an ordinary sort of guy."

Notes

1. General Chuck Yeager and Charles Leerhsen, *Press On: Further Adventures in the Good Life* (New York, Bantam Books, 1988), p. 98.
    On October 14, 1997, fifty years to the day after Chuck Yeager first broke the sound barrier, he repeated the feat in an F-15 Eagle. At 30,000 feet over Edwards AFB, at 10:34 A.M. (the altitude and time of his old record), he exceeded Mach 1. He was seventy-four. Afterward, asked about the significance of his role in breaking the sound barrier, Yeager replied with characteristic self-effacement: "I didn't fly the X-1 to leave a legacy, I did it because it was my duty."
    On October 15, 1997, fifty years and a day after Yeager's 1947 flight, a Royal Air Force pilot became the first man to break the sound barrier on the ground. Andy Green, a captain in the RAF, guided the jet-powered, twin-engine Thrust SSC to a record 763.035 miles per hour across the Nevada desert. His record speed—obtained on the second of two runs—surpassed Yeager's 1947 record by more than 63 MPH. A pilot pacing Thrust in an aircraft said twenty-foot-wide shockwaves were visible near the front wheels, caused by air pressure buildup. Nonetheless, the car ran straight and true—and so fast the sound it generated followed three to five miles behind!

2. Under the National Security Act of 1947, the Army Air Corps became the Air Force on September 18 of that year. Initiated by President Truman, this action was opposed by Navy leaders who feared they would lose control of maritime aviation.

3. Ken Gepfert, "Northrop Claims AF Scuttled 'Flying Wing'," *Los Angeles Times*, December 8, 1980, pp. 1, 21, 23.

4. Placed in a hangar at Long Beach, California, since its one and only flight, the Spruce Goose was disassembled in October 1992 and moved to McMinnville, Oregon, where—still in pieces—it was stored in a warehouse. As of mid-1998, the huge aircraft was still awaiting reassembly.

5. Francis K. Mason and Martin C. Windrow, *Air Facts and Feats: A Record of International Aerospace Achievement* (New York, Doubleday and Company, Inc., 1970), p. 191.

6. Curt Sutherly, "Ken Arnold—First American Pilot to Report UFOs," *Saga's UFO Report*, March 1977, pp. 42–43, 62, 64–65, 70.

7. Smith and a co-pilot, Ralph Stevens, spotted nine flying discs on July 4, 1947 just after the two had taken off from the airport in Boise, Idaho. Their description of the discs was similar to Arnold's, but the July 4 objects flew in two groups of four and five each.

8. The anonymous telephone caller was probably a third party acting in collusion with Crisman and Dahl. One or both men may have been wearing a "wire"—an electronic eavesdropping device—that allowed conversation in the hotel room to be monitored and/or recorded by a third individual. This would account for the anonymous messages telephoned to newspaper reporters even while Crisman and Dahl were both present in the hotel room.

9. John A. Keel, "The Maury Island Caper," *UFOs: 1947–1987*, compiled and edited by Hilary Evans with John Spencer for the British UFO Research Association (1987), pp. 40–43.

CHAPTER 2

Something Odd
Is Going On

THE "FLYING SAUCER" summer of 1947 came to a close, but the events of the summer—particularly the Kenneth Arnold sighting—lived on as legend. People everywhere were debating the existence of a heretofore little-known phenomenon, the UFO.

Various theories arose to explain the nature and origin of the mysterious objects, but because of their speed and maneuverability and the apparent intelligence behind those actions, the notion that UFOs were vehicles from another world quickly moved to the forefront of public awareness. By early 1949, the spacecraft explanation had thoroughly wormed its way into the American psyche. As a consequence, the U.S. Air Force—charged with defense of the nation's airspace—found itself committed to a long-term investigation of the phenomenon. The effort, time-consuming and ultimately futile for a variety of reasons, gradually became a public relations nightmare.

The summer of 1952 was something of a watershed for UFO activity, with anomalous objects appearing on radar over the

U.S. capital. The targets—on three separate radarscopes (two at Washington National Airport and one at nearby Andrews AFB) and corroborated by ground and aircraft observation—were tracked at speeds ranging from one hundred to 7,000 miles per hour.[1] The radar sets were subsequently found free of mechanical defect.

The Washington, D.C., sightings occurred on the weekends of July 19–20 and July 26–27, and caused channels of communication to be jammed with traffic about UFOs. The ensuing flap was so intense that intelligence personnel became concerned that the Soviets might be able to employ UFO activity as a basis for psychological warfare. With this in mind, a secret panel of scientists was convened the following January, headed by a physicist and CIA employee named H. P. Robertson.[2] The panel recommended a "debunking" campaign to scale-down public interest in UFOs, and thereby defuse a presumably dangerous situation. The Air Force, meanwhile, was taking repeated hits from both the news media and civilian investigators, with the media demanding an explanation and the civilians charging cover-up.

Debunking efforts notwithstanding, UFO sightings continued to intrigue well into the 1950s. In the late summer and fall of 1957, a second dramatic flap engaged the nation. The flap persisted into 1958, but by year's end much of the activity had shifted abroad, with subsequent reports coming from France, South America, Great Britain, and Scandinavia. The following year, 1959, sighting reports in the U.S. decreased even more significantly, although by this time the government's debunking campaign—which had finally begun to take hold—may have been partly responsible for the decline.

★ ★ ★

On April 24, 1964, a police officer was pursuing a speeding vehicle on the outskirts of the town of Socorro, New Mexico, when he heard a roar and observed a bright light losing altitude in the southwest sky. The time was about 5:45 P.M.

Anomalous flying objects were reported over Washington, D.C., during two separate weekends in July 1952. Detected on radar scopes at Washington National Airport and at nearby Andrews AFB, the objects were also spotted by ground observers and by the pilots of aircraft attempting to intercept the UFOs. Above, a night view of **Air Force aircraft** on the flight line. (Photo by the author)

Alarmed because he knew a dynamite shack was located in the area of the descending light, Officer Lonnie Zamora aborted the chase and drove into the desert. He managed to coax his car to the top of a difficult incline where, in a gully not far away, he saw an object that he at first believed was an overturned vehicle. He quickly discovered that the object was not an automobile; it was egg-shaped or elliptical and rested on the sloped ground on four uneven legs. Two men dressed in white and somewhat short in stature stood alongside the object; when they saw Zamora they seemed startled and quickly disappeared from view.[3] A moment later the object ascended with a roar and whine. The entire occurrence lasted several minutes.[4]

Sergeant Sam Chavez, a state policeman, arrived soon thereafter and found Zamora pale and shaken. Other officers arrived and a site search and investigation was conducted. Four indentations in the ground were discovered where the legs or landing struts of the object had been visible. Charred greasewood brush was found, and the soil showed evidence of calcination or high heating. Zamora himself was so distraught that he insisted on visiting a priest before completing a written report of the incident.

Writers and investigators who were determined to cast doubt on the patrolman's credibility scrutinized Zamora's account. However, the fact that the initial investigation was conducted by trained police officers—the only personnel immediately on the scene—infused the affair with a veracity and professionalism seldom found in UFO landing or close encounter cases. Media coverage was intense and for a time the Socorro affair eclipsed most other news stories. No one suspected that the incident marked the beginning of a new round of intense sighting activity, that by the end of the following year, UFOs would be reported in unprecedented numbers over nearly every continent of the globe.[5]

★ ★ ★

The Lonnie Zamora sighting was, for me, a catalyst. I was thirteen years old—a junior-high-school student with an interest in science and literature, and a growing enthusiasm for anything having to do with UFOs. The Socorro story pushed this to a new level. In school, hardly a week passed that I wasn't embroiled in an argument with fellow students, or even teachers, about the nature of the UFO phenomenon. Most of my friends thought the objects were either optical illusions or the product of wild imagination, but they somehow tolerated my outspokenness. Others, less kindly disposed, simply decided that my own imagination had taken a turn for the worse.

One of my science teachers, Jackson Underkoffler, was more sympathetic. He encouraged my interest while cautioning me to temper my enthusiasm with logic and objectivity. He pointed out that the objects might not be spacecraft—as was being suggested by the more sensational news accounts, and by many civilian researchers—but that they might be natural phenomena or something entirely new and unknown. At one point he loaned me a hefty report prepared by the National Investigations Committee on Aerial Phenomena (NICAP). Headed by Donald E. Keyhoe, a retired Marine major, NICAP was at the time the country's leading civilian UFO research organization. I kept the report for weeks before finally returning it.

Throughout the remainder of 1964 and into 1965, UFO activity mounted steadily in locations around the world. The lid came off in July 1965.

On July 2, 1965, members of an English base in Antarctica watched a huge UFO maneuver overhead.[6] On July 3, personnel at the Chilean and Argentine bases on the South Orkney Islands, north of the Antarctic landmass, reported a UFO. Instruments at the Argentine base designed to record magnetic field activity measured a strong, sudden disturbance as the object passed overhead.[7] That same day, on Deception Island at the west end of Antarctica, members of a base maintained by the Argentine Navy watched a giant lens-shaped flying object as it changed color, speed, and direction.[8] The object was almost identical in description to the UFO reported by personnel at the English base. On July 11, a number of huge disc-shaped objects were sighted over Portugal. The same day a luminous white object was spotted over the Azores Islands.[9] Other sightings during the period occurred in Europe, Africa, Australia . . . and North America.

In the United States and Mexico, UFOs were reported coast to coast. By the end of July 1965 a flap was in full swing over North America. By August the mood regarding UFOs—the emotional climate—had become charged: literally tens of thousands of North Americans had experienced the phenomenon, and for them at least there was no denying that something very odd was going on.[10]

* * *

On July 13, 1965—the day after my fifteenth birthday, at about 12:15 P.M., a UFO was spotted in Lebanon County, Pennsylvania, not far from my parents' home. The object remained in view until about 4:00 P.M. Eyewitness accounts, telephoned to police and to the local media, suggested that the UFO was "circular" and "metallic." Other reports said it changed in color, from red to blue or white, and also changed shape (a UFO characteristic we will examine in a later chapter). The object appeared to be moving slowly southwest, out of the area.

Reacting to the many calls and reports, an editor for the regional newspaper telephoned the public affairs office at Olmstead AFB near Harrisburg, twenty miles west in neighboring Dauphin County, and demanded an explanation.[11] Base personnel responded by dispatching a jet fighter. Within minutes the pilot radioed that he had spotted the object, which he said appeared to be a large "clear plastic balloon in the process of inflating."[12] At 17,000 feet the pilot broke off pursuit. Witnesses on the ground said the object accelerated when the aircraft arrived. Atmospheric conditions were reported to be good, with a high ceiling and extended visibility. Olmstead officials later admitted that they were unable to confirm the presence of a large balloon in the area that day.

Ten days later, in Pittsburgh at the western end of the state, several witnesses reported a silvery flying object "with a rocket-like orange tail." Meanwhile, across the Atlantic, the residents of Warminster, England were being blasted by strange "sonic waves."

The attacks on Warminster began in December 1964 and coincided with a sudden and spectacular UFO flap in the area.[13] According to news accounts, the townspeople were convinced that the attacks were orchestrated by the UFOs. In one instance, a woman was reportedly thrown against a wall by "savage sound waves." In another, a young girl was paralyzed by sounds waves while a UFO was visible nearby. Equally strange were reports of "giant thistles" that came "whistling" out of the sky. Rodents, pigeons, and other small animals were found dead nearly every day—killed by high-frequency sound waves. The attacks continued on and off for more than six months, until July 1965, ending only after the Warminster UFO sightings had ceased.

Back in the states, the wave of UFO activity hit an all-time high on the night of August 2–3, 1965. That night, residents throughout much of the Midwest and Southwest stood outside their homes or alongside their automobiles, watching wave after wave of brightly colored objects dart across the dark skies. In Texas, Colorado, and in the Great Plains states the activity was strongest. Police, newspaper offices, and radio and television stations were flooded with calls from eyewitnesses.

The following morning an Air Force spokesman asserted, in a national press statement, that the sightings were nothing more than the misidentification of four bright stars—Rigel, Betelgeuse, Aldebaran, and Capella. The stars are located in the constellations Orion, Taurus, and Auriga. The assertion triggered a howl of public protest, as well as an immediate rebuttal from respected members of the astronomy community. Among the respondents were Walter Webb, chief lecturer at the Hayden Planetarium in Boston, and Dr. Robert Risser of the Oklahoma Science and Art Planetarium. Webb pointed out that the four stars and their constellations are visible in August "only from the other side of the world." Dr. Risser concurred, noting that the "Air Force assertion . . . is about as far from the truth as you can get."[14]

* * *

Nine days later, on August 11, 1965, near Monroe, Michigan, a teenage girl was reportedly attacked by a hairy, upright monster that reached through an open car window.[15] The incident, although not linked to any known UFO activity, is noteworthy here because of its bizarre nature and the fact that it occurred at the height of the 1965 flap.

Wire services identified the victim—who was also the driver of the car—as seventeen-year-old Christine Van Acker. The girl's mother, Rose Owen, was a passenger. News reports were somewhat

conflicted, but the essential details noted that Van Acker was nego-
tiating a curve when a creature—seven feet tall and hairy—reportedly stepped onto the road, causing her to brake in panic. An instant
later the creature reached through the open car window. "I looked
over," Mrs. Owen said, "and there was this huge hairy hand on top
of her [Christine's] head." A commotion ensued, with both women
screaming and Van Acker repeatedly sounding the car horn. The
creature retreated back into the woods. The two were discovered a
few moments later by David Thomas, twenty-two, who said he
investigated after hearing the car horn. He found Owen "standing
on the road south of the car and Christine draped over the steering
wheel."[16] Van Acker sustained facial bruises during the encounter,
and her photo was published in newspapers and magazines across
the country.

The entire episode might have been summarily dismissed or
explained away were it the only such occurrence of its kind; but
"hairy giant" reports had been numerous in Michigan during June
and July 1965, and the month of August was proving no different.
Christine Van Acker's terrifying experience succeeded in drawing
the attention of the national media. As word spread and other witnesses came forward with their own stories, residents became concerned, then alarmed. Local authorities were left to deal with the
inevitable reactionary fallout—in this case a vigilante "posse" that
nearly escalated events out of control.

Armed with firearms and makeshift weapons, the members of the
posse searched the wooded countryside but found nothing. They
believed the creature was a radiation-spawned mutation from the
nearby Enrico Fermi Atomic Power Plant. The station had gone
on-line only a few years earlier, and the posse proposed a search of
the plant grounds. For a time the situation grew tense. Plant opera-
tors responded by locking the gates and adding extra guards.[17]

Roads into the area, meanwhile, were jammed with sightseers
and newly arrived monsters hunters, as were restaurants, gas stations, and motor lodges. The commotion proved a godsend for

establishment owners and managers. Said one drive-in restaurant owner: "I don't care what [the creature] is as long as it stays around."[18]

* * *

Harold Butcher, sixteen, was milking cows on his parents' farm in Cherry Creek, New York, when his transistor radio was disrupted by static. It was August 19, 1965, eight days after the reported attack on Christine Van Acker. The milking machine—powered by a tractor engine—suddenly halted and a bull tethered outside the barn bellowed and panicked. Looking out a window, Harold saw a large elliptical object land about a quarter-mile away. The object emitted a smell of burned gasoline and a red vapor clouded its rim. A strange beeping sound was heard. The object departed by ascending straight up into the clouds. Family members found damaged grass and two depressions in the ground at the apparent landing site.[19]

On September 21, 1965, UFOs were back in Pennsylvania. Two brothers, Ronald, twenty-three, and Gary, eighteen, were traveling in separate cars to their Lebanon County home when they spotted something over the road.[20] The time was about 10:30 P.M. Arriving at the house, they called their sisters, Susan, fifteen, and Kay, twenty, and a visiting friend, Becky, to the front lawn. For several minutes they stood outside and watched a strange flying object rimmed with green lights. The UFO vanished, only to be sighted by Ronald rising out of a copse of trees behind the house. The object spun around a few times before disappearing back into the trees.

At the time of the incident, the parents of the four siblings were asleep and didn't learn of the UFO until the next day. The neighbors were awake, however, and were summoned outside by the boys. They all got a look at the object before it vanished a final time.

The following night, September 22, 1965, a Lebanon County motorist and his girlfriend, who was a passenger in the car, spotted a disc-shaped UFO. The witnesses—Larry, twenty-two, a resident of the borough of Cleona, and Gail, twenty, of nearby Annville—said they first noticed the object in the southwestern sky where it appeared to tilt toward the ground over an open field. The object then moved west toward Hershey, Pennsylvania. The two kept the UFO in view until they arrived at Gail's house, where she summoned her father.

Soon, some thirty people were gathered in front of the house watching the UFO.[21] One enterprising youngster—a fourteen-year-old named Michael—located a 30 x 40 power telescope and set it up for a better view. He later told a reporter: "I don't know what a flying saucer is supposed to look like, but this thing had a white dome on top and another on the bottom and there was a ring of red and green lights zigzagging around it." Another witness, a housewife, said the lights of the UFO "flickered on and off." She said a commercial airliner passed overhead and the UFO "shot out a red flame and took out after the airplane;" but the UFO followed only briefly before returning to its previous position.

Someone in the group decided to telephone the local newspaper, the *Lebanon Daily News*. A staff photographer, hereafter identified as "PW," responded to the scene.[22] Years later, in September 1974, I spoke with the photographer about the incident.[23]

PW told me the newsroom had received a call about a small crowd of people watching "strange lights" over Annville. "When I got there," he said, "the thing was pretty high and wouldn't have shown up on a photograph. I watched it until it got that far out that it looked like a star. I know it all sounds pretty funny, but I also know there was a thing up there that appeared out of the ordinary."

PW said he tried to photograph the object through the lens of the telescope—a nearly impossible feat without a mounting bracket for the camera. "Every time I tried to focus and would finally get set up, the object would move one way or another. Then I'd have to focus all over again. It was frustrating," he said. "I had my telephoto lens with me, but it wasn't powerful enough to get a shot at that thing."

Eventually the UFO disappeared to the west, only to be replaced by another coming from the north. The second object was joined by still another (or possibly it was the first one returning) and then both objects vanished for good.

★ ★ ★

That same night, northeast of Annville in the Lebanon County village of Fredericksburg, Dale E. Richard and his father, Elmer, were drinking coffee in the Fredericksburg Diner when a truck driver rushed in to report a fire on the grounds of the nearby speedway. The news was of immediate concern to Richard for two reasons: he was both the area fire chief and the owner of the speedway.

Accompanied by several men, father and son hurried to the speedway but found no fire, indeed they found nothing out of the ordinary—until the next morning, that is, when Richard, along with several racetrack employees, discovered a circle burned in the grassy infield, seven feet in diameter and perfectly round. Equally spaced around the circle were four marks or impressions, as if something on legs or struts had rested there.

The following day, details of the incident reached the county editor's desk at the *Lebanon Daily News*. Once again, PW was the photographer on duty.

During the aforementioned interview, he said: "No blow torch could have done what we saw at the track. The grass was burned only in the circle. The grass outside [the circle] was all right."[24]

PW's observation was prompted, in part, by a widely held suspicion that Richard had manufactured the infield burn in order to publicize his auto-racing venture. I was aware of this suspicion because I had grown up in the town, and for many years I too was skeptical about the origin of the burned circle. My talk with PW forced me to reconsider.

On September 17, 1974, I visited Dale Richard at his automotive repair shop at the site of the Fredericksburg Speedway, long since closed. I handed him a photocopy of a newspaper story about the incident, and asked if he recalled the events of that night in September 1965. He studied the story for a minute, looked up and said, "Yes, it happened just like it says here. I have no explanation for what happened."[25] When I remarked that there were many in the town that still believed the story was a publicity stunt, Richard said nothing at all. But he maintained eye contact; he never looked away. And his solemn, sober expression never changed.

★ ★ ★

The UFO flap of 1965 continued into the fall.

Winter arrived, and in December a high-school pal, Elmer Benjamin Weaver, asked me to assist in releasing a dozen or more Midwestern cottontails into the fields north of Fredericksburg.[26] The rabbits had been trucked in from Kansas by his father's rod and gun club, and the idea was to release them back into the wild in the hope that they would survive and breed—creating additional wild game for Pennsylvania hunters. Experiments of this sort are usually doomed to failure—predators usually kill the transplanted animals before they have a chance to adjust to the new terrain. The members of the rod and gun club were aware of this, aware of the low chance for success, but hoped nonetheless that some of the cottontails would adapt and survive.

The Weaver home was only a few blocks from my parents' house, and so on a cold winter evening Ben and I found ourselves lugging a pair of large rabbit cages along a road that led north out of town. The rabbits were nervous, and kept shuffling around. We were forced to stop often to adjust our grip on the cages.

Darkness had arrived and a light snow was falling. Our conversation, as I recall, was largely about our plans for Christmas vacation, only a couple of weeks away.

As we walked, we discovered that several domestic cats, intent on the rabbits, were following us. Each time we stopped to rest, Ben would shout at the cats in the hope of chasing them away.

They stayed close, however, and it seemed obvious that at least some of the rabbits were destined to become tender tidbits. We finally reached a point a mile north of town where we stepped off the road into an open field. Ben opened the cage doors, and as the cottontails fled we did our best to run interference against the pursuing cats. When the rabbits were out of sight, we picked up the cages and returned to the road.

The snowfall had intensified and visibility was limited. Retracing our path, we discussed the fate of the cottontails—wondering how many, if any, would survive.

In the sky directly ahead, two bright red lights appeared. They moved side by side at a low altitude, coming our way—clearly visible through the veil of snow. I glanced at Ben, he at me. Neither of us spoke. The only sound was the faint swish of falling snow.

As the lights drew near, I had the distinct feeling that these were not separate objects but were opposite points of some shape in-between. What's more, I was fairly certain this was not a conventional aircraft. Ben and I had grown up around airplanes—a small grass-covered airfield was situated at the west end of town. The planes that flew out of that field had red, green, and amber position lights, were noisy, and were not aloft in near-zero visibility.

The approaching lights, whatever they were, were eerie and different. They passed overhead without a sound, traveling more slowly than any aircraft I had ever heard of except lighter-than-air: a balloon or a blimp, and I was certain these lights were neither. They flew north into the curtain of snow, headed toward the mountains, and we watched them fade.

Safely back home, I told my parents about the eerie red lights. They listened politely, and concluded that Ben and I had witnessed an aircraft gliding with the engine on idle. I didn't accept that then, and still don't today. Whatever the red lights were they were strange and unknown—a UFO for want of a better term—and they inspired a combination of awe and fear that has stayed with me through all the years since.

Notes

1. Edward J. Ruppelt, *The Report on Unidentified Flying Objects* (New York, Doubleday, 1956), pp. 156–172.

2. Frederick C. Durant, "Report of Meeting of Scientific Advisory Panel on Unidentified Flying Objects Convened by Office of Scientific Intelligence, CIA (January 14–18, 1953)." The twenty-five-page summary, also known as the Robertson Panel Report, or more frequently the "Durant Report," was declassified December 18, 1974. The author received a copy along with appended documents and a detailed cover letter from Gene F. Wilson, CIA information and privacy coordinator, in response to a January 1976 inquiry.

3. During an interview with Patrick Huyghe, published in *The Anomalist*, issue number eight, 2000, Lonnie Zamora said that he no longer believed he actually saw two men outside the grounded UFO—that he only thought he did at the time. In a footnote, Huyghe states that two hours after the Socorro incident, an FBI agent told Zamora that it would be better if Zamora didn't mention seeing the two small figures because no one would believe him.

4. Keith Thompson, *Angels and Aliens* (New York, Fawcett Columbine Books, 1993), pp. 74–77; also Jacques and Janine Vallee, *Challenge to Science: The UFO Enigma* (Chicago, Henry Regnery Company, 1966), pp. 34–35.

5. A wealth of information on the UFO occurrences of 1964 is offered in *The Forgotten Flap*—a thirty-page booklet by Rick R. Hilberg. Published in early 2000, *The Forgotten Flap* provides detailed, straightforward documentation of UFO sightings from October 1963 through December 1964, with nearly fifty reports covered in the volume. Of these reports, only the Lonnie Zamora sighting is well remembered—everything else during the year having been overshadowed by the more widely publicized occurrences of 1965 and 1966. The booklet is an excellent reference for anyone interested in the history of the UFO phenomenon. Further information can be obtained by writing Hilberg at 377 Race Street, Berea, Ohio 44017.

6. Frank Edwards, *Flying Saucers—Serious Business* (New York, Lyle Stuart Inc., 1966), p. 284.

7. Ibid., p. 283.

8. Ibid., p. 282.

9. Ibid., pp. 285–286.

10. To anyone not yet born or quite young at the time, the likelihood that "tens of thousands" of North Americans could have observed UFOs during the summer of 1965 must seem so unlikely an occurrence as to border on the absurd. Nonetheless, it is true. A check of the microfilm records of virtually any newspaper in any sizable city for the night of August 2–3, 1965 will provide a frame of reference for what transpired. What's more, published reports about UFOs tend only to scratch the surface: for every one person who observes and reports a UFO, expect that there are at least nine other witnesses who do not.

11. Olmstead AFB, Pennsylvania, was deactivated in the late 1960s and is today the site of Harrisburg International Airport and home to the 193rd Air National Guard Special Operations Wing.

12. Curt Sutherly, "Case History of a UFO Flap," *Official UFO*, December 1976, p. 41.

13. The events in Warminster, England, received wide publicity mainly due to the efforts of a newspaperman, Arthur Shuttlewood. Editor of the *Warminster Journal,* Shuttlewood ultimately published a book (*The Warminster Mystery,* London, Neville Spearman, 1967) about the bizarre and frightening events in the town. Shuttlewood's death at age eighty was noted in the January 10, 1998 issue of *Saucer Smear* (Vol. 45, No. 1), published by James W. Moseley. About Shuttlewood, Moseley said: "He believed that Warminster attracted UFOs because it was on a straight line between the ancient holy sites of Stonehenge and Glastonbury. He was once quoted as saying that UFOs 'could be shadows of our future, time travelers, or astral entities that have come to warn us of what to beware of in years to come . . .'"

14. Frank Edwards, *Flying Saucers—Serious Business* (New York, Lyle Stuart Inc., 1966) p. 291; also Sutherly, "Case History of a UFO Flap," *Official UFO*, December 1976, p. 59.

15. Curt Sutherly, "UFOs and Manimals: A Nuclear Power Connection?," *Argosy UFO*, March 1977, pp. 13, 50; also Sutherly, "Case

History Of a UFO Flap," *Official UFO*, December 1976, pp. 59–60; also Jerome Clark, *The Unexplained* (Detroit, Visible Ink Press, 1993), p. 170; also Gray Barker, "Atomic Monsters in Michigan," *Spacecraft News*, No. 1, November 1965.

16. Sutherly, "UFOs and Manimals: A Nuclear Power Connection," *Argosy UFO*, March 1977, p. 50.

17. Several months following the spate of monster sightings and related events near Monroe, Michigan, the Enrico Fermi Atomic Power Plant was temporarily shut down due to unexplained sabotage. Journalist John Fuller documented the incident in a book, *We Almost Lost Detroit*.

18. Sutherly, "Case History," *Official UFO*, December 1976, p. 60.

19. Richard Hall, *Uninvited Guests* (Santa Fe, Aurora Press, 1988), p. 254; also Keith Thompson, *Angels and Aliens* (New York, Fawcett Columbine, 1993), p. 79; also, Jacques Vallee, *Passport to Magonia* (Chicago, Contemporary Books, 1969) p. 314.

20. Sutherly, "Case History," *Official UFO*, December 1976, p. 60.

21. Ibid., pp. 61, 62.

22. The photographer quoted in this and subsequent passages died in 2000 following a protracted illness. I have identified him by middle and last initials only—a decision arrived at after learning of his death during a phone conversation with his widow.

23. Sutherly, "Case History," *Official UFO*, December 1976, pp. 61, 62.

24. Ibid., p. 62.

25. Ibid., p. 62.

26. As far as I can determine, the rabbits Ben and I released that winter night in 1965 were *Sylvilagus auduboni*—the desert cottontail. The rabbit inhabits areas of the West and Southwest, including western Kansas and Texas.

CHAPTER 3

Strangers
in the Night

DECEMBER 1965 GAVE way to January 1966. UFO sightings continued worldwide but not to the extent that was previously apparent. Looking back, the abatement in reports may have had more to do with diminished media interest and persistent government naysaying than any actual decline in UFO activity. Whatever the reason, the lull was not to last.

Activity soared in March 1966 with the infamous Michigan "swamp gas" debacle and settled into a steady stream of reports that continued through the summer.[1] The following year, the pattern reoccurred with a springtime escalation in sightings that lasted into the fall of 1967.

My own interest in the UFO phenomenon, while not exactly diminished at this time, was at least temporarily set aside. I was seventeen and working after school in order to make payments on a car. The remainder of my time was spent enjoying the newfound freedom of the road.

That summer the hometown fire company hosted the county firemen's parade and convention, and during the festivities several friends and I hatched a plan to go camping overnight in the mountains north of town. The site of our intended camp was the Little Mountain—a foothill of Blue Mountain, part of the Appalachian chain. In 1967 this area was more isolated than it is today, surrounded by farmland and woodland and accessible only by meandering country roads. Access to the mountain itself was along a narrow dirt road that looped back, creating a large circle.

I was familiar with the Little Mountain because I had hunted wild game there with my father, and I found the prospect of an overnight camp intriguing. My friends too were excited, and with the consent of our parents we packed food, tent, flashlights and sleeping bags, and set off in a couple of aging automobiles.

My camping pals included my cousin, Larry Zeigler; one of his close friends, Mike; a mutual friend, Joe; and my neighbors, Wayne Rentschler and Steve Hetrick. We arrived several hours before dark, selected a campsite and unloaded our gear. We planned no craziness that night—no drugs or alcohol, or for that matter even a loud radio—and anticipated no problems or uninvited guests. We had, in fact, told no one except our parents of our plans to enter the mountain, and the only visitors we thought at all likely were a few wild scavengers or predators, and nothing larger or more dangerous than a fox or a bobcat.

Our campsite was established only a short distance from where we parked the cars, but far enough into the timber so as to go unobserved from the road.[2] In fact, a better location could not have been found: the ground was reasonably level and not too stony, which meant sleeping would not be a problem, and a small stream trickled nearby, providing water for the camp. (In those days you could drink untreated mountain water without undue concern for your health.) We set up the tent and readied our sleeping bags, then prepared a fire. By nightfall we were ensconced comfortably in the forest.

I have observed through the years and during numerous camps in all sorts of country that sleep comes early in the wild. This may be an instinctive reversion to a more primitive behavior. Or it may simply be that when in the wild, one has no television or stereo or personal computer to occupy time and mind (unless, of course, you are one of those people who simply has to pack in a stereo boombox or a laptop PC, in which case you might as well remain at home). Free of high-tech trappings, there is an opportunity to make conversation with your fellow campers, or if not so inclined to simply listen to the night—marveling at the sounds you would otherwise never hear.

So it was on this night. We sat about the fire telling stories and talking youthful nonsense while roasting hot dogs and eating canned chili. Gradually the conversation waned as the food, coupled with the quiet sounds of the forest, lulled us. After a time we turned in—the others to the tent, I to a sleeping bag unrolled nearby.

★ ★ ★

I awoke to find the camp dark, the fire long since reduced to faint embers. Groping alongside the sleeping bag, I found my flashlight and used it to illuminate my watch: it was 3:00 A.M. Overhead in the trees, a great-horned owl called in a deep, eerie voice. I shivered in the sleeping bag. The owl's cry reminded me of a hunting hound baying at a distance.

Another sound—throbbing and faint—caught my attention. I switched off the light and crawled from the sleeping bag. Dressed in jeans, I slipped into my sneakers and pulled a T-shirt over my head. In the camp, all was still; only that faint, errant throb intruded on the silence of the wood. Not waking the others, I moved off in the direction of the access road. I stepped carefully amid the trees— unaccountably afraid to use the flashlight in my hand.

From overhead the owl called again, giving me a start. The bird seemed to be staying with me, marking my progress, and it occurred to me that with its remarkable night vision and higher vantage point the owl had already located the source of the sound—may in fact have been watching it all along.

My own vision was now adjusting to the dark and I could see the access road through the timber. I stopped and listened. The sound was coming from somewhere down the road. Slowly the throbbing grew louder until I recognized it as the sound of a car engine—a throaty V-8—turning over at low speed. I hunkered down in the forest. A moment later the glow of headlights filtered through the trees.

The car drew abreast of my hiding place and then, quite unexpectedly, stopped! The headlights darkened. A spotlight speared the night sky. I froze. The spotlight swung down and around and settled directly on the camp! Afraid even to breathe, I could hear my friends stirring in the tent.

A gunshot cracked in the night!

Pandemonium erupted within the tent, and I heard Wayne cry out and shout to the others to get down. Oddly, the sound of their terror dispelled my own paralysis, and on hands and knees I began moving toward the road—suddenly (and perhaps stupidly) determined to get a better view of the car.

As I edged forward, I heard the squawk of a two-way radio. Then the spotlight went out. Again I froze as the vehicle resumed motion without lighting its headlamps. Summoning what was left of my nerve, I pushed to the edge of the timber in time to see the car's dark shape disappear up the road.

Rising from my hiding place, I hurried back to the camp where I conferred with the others. No one had been hurt, but the level of fear was intense. We argued about who might be in the car. Cops, someone said, mentioning the gun and radio. That didn't make sense, I replied. Police would have announced themselves and they wouldn't have fired a gun without reason. Someone else—Larry, I believe—agreed with my reasoning, adding that the gunshot didn't sound like the report of a police issue but more like a light caliber—a .22 or .32 firearm.

If not cops, then who? Wayne demanded, insisting that it could have been the township police "having fun."

"Whoever they are, they'll be back," Mike pointed out. The fear we all felt was evident in his voice.

Mike was correct. The car would either turn around and retrace its path or would follow the loop and come out below us. Either way we had little time in which to decide a course of action, little time to elect whether to stay or flee. Uncertain, we argued and debated—and then it was too late. The car was already returning!

What each of us did or said at that moment I honestly don't recall. As it is, I am able to provide substantive detail only because I long kept notes. I do recall that I was seized by a kind of intellectual dysfunction: adrenaline kicked in and some lower instinct assumed control. Psychologists call this behavior a "fight or flight" response to a life-threatening circumstance—the behavior of a soldier in war, which is a fancy way of saying you want to save your own skin. I've been to this particular house of horrors on a number of occasions through the years, but that night in 1967 was a first. I was a kid, a boy. We were all boys, and boys are supposed to have fun, not face terror on a camping trip at three in the morning.

So we waited—hunkered down on the ground, using the trees as cover; waited for the spotlight to locate each and every one of us—waited for another gunshot to crack in the night. When you are a teenager the imagination is incredibly active, and I'm sure we all imagined the worst.

Time slowed. The car approached—its headlights off, engine grumbling. My heart pounded. Without any perceptible change in speed the car moved past and was gone.

We crept out of our respective cover and stood there, stunned. Then everyone started babbling. Out of this came a terse suggestion from Larry that we check our own cars to be certain they had not been damaged or entered.

Like a pack of panicked dogs, we fell out into the road and raced breakneck to the place where we had parked our vehicles. I was bringing up the rear when I heard someone up ahead stumble and fall. A lengthy curse followed, after which our flashlights told the story: a log—a dead tree—blocked the road. Beyond the barricade lay another, and beyond that another, undoubtedly put there by someone in the car. How the logs had been laid into place so quickly was a mystery, but it was not something that any of us pondered long, then and there. Checking the cars, we satisfied ourselves that nothing was amiss. Then we hauled the logs off the road.

Back in the camp we rekindled the fire and tossed on wood till it began to roar. The fear we all felt was beginning to diminish, replaced by a kind of angry jitters. As boys, we liked to believe we were fearless, but the events of the night were beyond anything in our youthful experience.

We remained at the camp until daybreak. Not one of us slept. We might have bolted except, I think, for a bizarre feeling that somewhere down the lane, beyond the trees, the car waited—the driver perhaps smiling in the darkness.

Daylight stole softly into the forest and we drowned the fire and packed up our gear. By the time we drove out of the mountain the sun had risen, and within a few days the events of the night faded in memory until they seemed like little more than a bad dream.

* * *

As frightening as our experience was that night, it was barely remarkable in comparison to events occurring elsewhere. A UFO flap—complete with nocturnal meandering lights, occupants, and strange creatures—had again spread across the nation. The bizarre activity was perhaps strongest in the Ohio River Valley, where it persisted for nearly fourteen months, from November 1966 to December 1967. John Keel later documented these events in his compelling book, *The Mothman Prophecies*.[3]

Perhaps the earliest occurrence in the Ohio Valley during this time was the widely publicized encounter between a salesman

Gray Barker, author and ufologist, at a UFO convention in New York City in 1980. Barker's books included *The Silver Bridge*, an account of the 1967 UFO/strange creature occurrences in and around Point Pleasant, West Virginia. (Photo by Michael G. Mann from the R. Hilberg collection)

named Woodrow Derenberger and a grinning UFO occupant. The occupant, a normal looking man who identified himself only as Mr. "Cold," spoke with Derenberger via telepathy before departing in his UFO. The incident—witnessed by other individuals—occurred on November 2, 1966, outside Parkersburg, West Virginia, and was reported to police. Thirteen days later, a menacing creature began appearing in and around the town of Point Pleasant, West Virginia. Dubbed "Mothman" by members of the media, the creature was described by witnesses as six to seven feet tall with large wings and glowing red eyes.

The arrival of Mothman was heralded not only by lurid media accounts but also by an outbreak of unexplained animal deaths and missing pets. In one case investigated by the late author Gray Barker, a German shepherd named Bandit vanished near Salem, West Virginia.[4] Bandit's owner, Newell Partridge, told Barker that on the night of November 14, 1966, the television set in the

Partridge house began to whine like a generator scaling up, while outside, Bandit began to wail. Partridge directed a flashlight toward the barn and observed two large red circles or "eyes." Bandit gave chase and when the dog failed to return, Partridge slept with a loaded gun by his side. The next morning he found Bandit's tracks where he had seen the "eyes." The tracks moved in a circle, as though the dog had been chasing his tail, and ended at that location.

Thirteen months later, on December 15, 1967, the seven-hundred-foot Silver Bridge at Point Pleasant collapsed during rush-hour traffic. Said one witness: "I looked up and it was gone. . . . The whole bridge had disappeared into the river."[5] A total of thirty-one vehicles plunged into the icy Ohio River, and forty-six people died in the tragedy.

On December 22, a week after the bridge disaster, Keel reported that a pair of strange men with olive complexions and dressed in black overcoats entered the office of the local newspaper correspondent, Mary Hyre.[6] Exhausted from the tragic events of the preceding week, Mrs. Hyre was perplexed when the men asked about UFO activity in the area. A weird conversation ensued during which one of the two asked what she would do if ordered to stop writing about flying saucers.

Later that day another man with dark eyes and a dark complexion entered her office and identified himself as Jack Brown, a UFO investigator. Another odd conversation followed, during which "Brown" claimed to be a friend of Gray Barker and asked questions about John Keel. Mrs. Hyre said the man spoke with an odd stammer and wore an ill-fitting, slightly old-fashioned suit. He wore no overcoat, despite the intense cold outside.

*　*　*

Characters such as "Jack Brown" have been annoying and frightening people for centuries. In earlier ages they were associated with the occult or with religious experience . . . the "dark men" of countless traditions. Today they are part of the UFO mythos. They arrive after a UFO or fortean event, sometimes afoot, sometimes driving automobiles that appear new even if the vehicle is clearly many years old. Often they arrive before the percipient has had a chance to report his or her experience. Sometimes they approach the friends or relatives of witnesses and investigators. They ask strange questions and make outlandish observations, or they simply follow from place to place. Their demeanor is unpleasant and their words and actions are often completely absurd.

I first learned of the "Men In Black" around 1969 or 1970 from stories in newsstand magazines and from a book written by Gray Barker.[7] Initially it all seemed like so much UFO-related paranoia. Soon, however, I was corresponding with both Keel and Barker, and each assured me that the MIB were a real if elusive phenomena. Not long after, I met Barker at a convention in Cleveland, and during a protracted conversation was reminded of that frightening night in the mountains in 1967. I outlined the experience for him and suggested that perhaps it was a MIB occurrence. Barker listened politely, and then cautioned that the episode was probably nothing more than an ordinary if somewhat extreme prank. Years later, I realized the irony of his response when I learned that Barker, along with his friend James Moseley, had managed to foist several impressive pranks and at least one serious hoax on the UFO community.[8]

Despite Barker's suggestion of a prank (or perhaps because of it), I found myself dwelling again on the events of that night in 1967. And the more I thought about it, the more I suspected a fortean experience. Consider: there was the owl—a bird associated with legend, including the legend of the wailing ghost, the "Banshee."[9] There was the curious way in which the occupant or occupants of the car seemed to know exactly where the camp was located. There was the matter of the log obstruction, placed across the road with what seemed (to me, at least) uncanny speed and silence. (Our campsite was not very distant and we should have heard the sound of dragging timber.) Finally, there was the intense, almost unnatural fear that accompanied the experience.

* * *

As I pursued my study of UFOs into the 1970s, I continued to hear about the Men In Black. The stories came from a variety of sources, including friends and acquaintances. I discovered that there were two distinct types of MIB: the secretive but otherwise (from all outward appearances) very human kind, and another variety which, based on the reports, seemed to be something else entirely . . . something not human but "parahuman." An example of the latter was reported to me in June 1977.

I had been away on a weekend trip, and on returning stopped at a small restaurant I routinely visited. The waitress on duty was a friend who knew of my interest in fortean events, and she observed that it was unfortunate I had not been present a day earlier.

A man, a stranger, she said, had approached the diner's main entrance and begun pushing futilely on the glass door. Clearly not understanding that he needed to pull in order to open the door, the man continued pushing until the waitress finally shouted "pull." She said the man wore an old work shirt and trousers, and she described him as middle-aged. He had dark skin (not black) and walked with an oddly stiff gait. She noted that there was something "eerie" about the man, something she could not quite define. In a village where strangers were a rarity, this man was especially peculiar.

Approaching the counter with an oddly fixed stare, the man asked the waitress for fifty cents. Thinking she had heard incorrectly, she ignored his request. When he asked again, she politely informed him that restaurants are in the business of making money, not giving it away. He responded with a brilliant "Oh!" and took a seat at the counter. He then asked for a glass of water. He apparently did not see, or did not recognize, the full glass the waitress had already placed in front of him. She pointed to the glass, which he picked up and emptied thirstily. Without another word the man stood and walked out of the restaurant, only to stare in at her for a long moment before moving on.

The man's bizarre actions and appearance unnerved my friend, but the strangest thing about him, she said, was that he never blinked! She admitted that he might have done so while she wasn't watching, but not once did she actually see his eyelids move.

An equally strange episode transpired in 1967 in an area with a long history of UFO and fortean phenomena—Colorado's San Luis Valley.[10] The percipient, who we'll refer to as Mrs. B., was an artist who had spotted a crescent-shaped object flying over the valley's Great Sand Dunes National Monument. She later painted the UFO, setting her memory of the experience to canvas.

Weeks later, Mrs. B. was visited at her home near Alamosa by a man inquiring about her painting. The visitor, who appeared to be about thirty-five, behaved oddly and declared that he was from a different universe. "I cannot read," he said, "but mention any book in any library and I will be able to tell you its contents." Unnerved by the stranger, Mrs. B. asked how he had learned about her painting. Instead of answering the question, the stranger simply reminded her that he could not read. He then confounded her further by asserting that humans waste too much time and energy in pursuit of food "when it could all be so easily taken from the atmosphere."

Mrs. B. told police that the man appeared to be physically ill. She said he insisted on buying the painting so she deliberately set a high price, to which the stranger replied that he had no money. The visitor departed in a car bearing Arizona registration, and months later police had still not managed to trace the plates.

To say that Mrs. B.'s visitor demonstrated a form of behavior that was both strange and irrational is to understate the issue, and the same is certainly true of the man in the restaurant. This is not to say, however, that either of these encounters was without design or purpose. In each instance the visitor inflicted a degree of mental confusion that forced the percipient to rethink fundamental views and beliefs, particularly parochial views about life and reality. Psychologists know this as the "confusion technique"—a form of mental reframing. It is an approach that opens the door to new ideas and possibilities, and if applied on a broad enough scale could, in theory, affect social change.

At the height of his interest in UFO and fortean phenomena, my friend Raymond may have had this obscure and unusual technique employed against him. This occurred during an odd MIB-like experience in his hometown. He described the encounter in a note appended to a letter dated August 16, 1976:

> On the way to mail the letter to you this noon, I passed through the hallway of a small office building cum drugstore . . . and there sitting on a bench in the hall was an old man in a business suit. Just as I approached he said, loud and clear, "Are you up there now?" As you can imagine I did a double take, but soon realized that he was not talking to me (although there was nobody else around). Exactly as if he were carrying on a conversation over the phone, he continued loud and clear: "Oh, you are up there! Good! I'll be there in a few minutes." With that he stood and walked out of the building and down the street.
>
> I had to choose between following him or walking the opposite direction to the post office. Sorry to relate, I went to the post office to mail your letter instead. Maybe I did the right thing: If I had followed the old gent, probably I would now be "up there" not knowing how to get down!

Despite its humorous quality, Raymond's story is similar to other MIB accounts in at least one important way: the stranger seemed drunk or disoriented (or in this case perhaps merely senile)—uttering apparent nonsense and appearing out of synch with his surroundings.

* * *

Not all Men In Black cases are quite so bizarre. As already noted, sometimes the encounter is with one or more individuals who seem entirely normal except that they behave mysteriously or secretively. They behave like covert agents, or like persons role-playing the part.

In 1965, following a low-level UFO event, the photographer PW was approached by a pair of men traveling in a black Plymouth. The men claimed to represent an organization studying UFOs. They asked for the location of several tall trees burned by the object (described as a classic disc) and said they needed bark and leaf samples for lab analysis. When PW pointed out the location, which was nearby, one of the men removed a pair of spiked shoes from the car and climbed into a tree. While this occurred, PW questioned the second man, but could extract no worthwhile information. The pair departed as soon as they had their samples.[11]

On May 23, 1964, in northwestern England near the border of Scotland, Jim Templeton, his wife and two daughters were spending the afternoon on the Burgh marsh along the Solway Firth (Solway estuary). Templeton, of Carlisle, England, was a camera buff. His five-year-old daughter, Elizabeth, was wearing a new dress, so he decided to take her picture. As he focused on his subject, he could see the cooling towers of the Chapelcross atomic energy plant across the estuary. Nothing else intruded on the camera's field of view, which he later reflected was odd as grazing sheep were normally scattered about the landscape. On this occasion, however, the sheep were all huddled together as if frightened.

Templeton took his exposed color film to a shop for processing. When he picked it up, the female manager at the shop commented on the "lovely" photo of his daughter, but expressed curiosity about "the big fellow" in the background. To his great surprise, Templeton discovered a second image in the photo—a man wearing a silver suit.

Teenage ufologist Rick Hilberg (left) with the late Donald E. Keyhoe in Cleveland in 1964. A retired Marine major, Keyhoe headed the National Investigations Committee on Aerial Phenomena (NICAP), and authored a number of successful UFO books, including *The Flying Saucers Are Real* (1950) and *Flying Saucers from Outer Space* (1953). (Photo by Allan Manak from the R. Hilberg collection)

Templeton's photo was published worldwide and examined by experts, who were baffled. The resulting media coverage attracted droves of UFO investigators, spiritualists, and curiosity seekers. Templeton was accused of perpetrating a hoax, which he insisted was nonsense. An employee of the Carlisle city fire brigade, he received a visit at the fire station one day from a pair of tall strangers riding in a black Jaguar limousine. The two, dressed in dark suits and bowler hats, identified themselves as government investigators and asked Templeton to accompany them to the Burgh marsh.[12] He described their attitude as "stand-offish and snooty." When they arrived at the marsh one of the men asked: "Is this where you saw the spaceman?" Templeton replied—as he had so many times before—that neither he nor any member of his family saw anyone at the time; they had been alone on the marsh. Upon hearing this, the two men climbed back into their Jag and drove away . . . leaving Templeton stranded at the marsh, six miles from Carlisle.

There is a postscript, of sorts, to this story: a few hours after Jim Templeton snapped his photo on the Burgh marsh, the countdown was halted for the launch of a test rocket in Woomera, Australia. According to reports at the time, a strange, silver-suited figure was seen in the launch area but was never located. When descriptions of the figure were compared with the image in the Templeton photo, the two proved to be virtually identical.

★　★　★

Strictly speaking, the next report has nothing to do with Men In Black, though it does involve a mystery man as well as a story about a crashed UFO. Compiled by Rick R. Hilberg, the account originally appeared in the now defunct *UFO Journal*.[13]

Hilberg, who resides with his wife and son in Berea, Ohio, near Cleveland, is a veteran ufologist and an authority on fortean phenomena.[14] In 1981 he received a telephone call from a man who said he wanted to report a UFO. The caller—identified here only as John—described a "daylight disc" performing acute aerial maneuvers. "I listened to his account," Hilberg said, "and politely informed him that we had many like it in our files."

John asked a good many questions, and at one point expressed interest in whether investigators in the Cleveland area had heard stories about crashed UFOs, and if so, whether they placed any credence in such tales. He then related a story of his own, claiming that he had never discussed it with anyone, not even with members of his own family, for fear they would think him a liar. The following summary is from the *UFO Journal* report, with the permission of Rick Hilberg:

> John was in a downtown Cleveland stamp shop [in August 1952] when he struck up a conversation with another customer. He said the two discussed stamps for a while, and generally seemed to enjoy each other's company. John described his new friend as a heavy-set man of about thirty-two, with a sort of dark complexion

and a crew cut. [For the sake of expediency the man is identified hereafter as "Robert," though his real name—if indeed the man ever existed—is not known.]

During the next several weeks . . . the two would meet at John's house to discuss stamps and sometimes play a few games of chess. John said his new friend would win every game even though John himself was a pretty fair chess player. He said he felt [at the time] as if Robert could read his mind because he always seemed to know John's next several moves. . . .

Robert claimed [to be] a chemical engineer for the state of Ohio. . . . He seemed to know a great deal about technical subjects. [He] would suddenly start rattling off all kinds of detailed information about a [particular] car, or about some complicated piece of machinery . . . It seemed as if Robert knew more about most any technical subject than even an engineer would know. He always spoke textbook perfect English, and although he claimed to be from Ohio he had a slight accent that John couldn't place.

About three weeks into their friendship, John was invited over to Robert's house for dinner and an evening of chess. . . . After dinner, John said Robert removed a photograph from a drawer and handed it to him, asking whether he had ever heard about flying objects. John replied that he didn't know much, but had read reports in the newspaper from time to time. John said he looked at the photograph and was amazed. [The image in the photo] appeared to be some sort of large machine crashed into the side of a hill.

Whatever it was, it was badly damaged by the crash . . . Parts of its outer skin were shredded and lying all over the crash site, and only a badly twisted frame remained that reminded him of an umbrella shape. John was certain, however, that whatever it was, [the object] wasn't any sort of aircraft he was familiar with. He said that two bodies were lying on the ground near the craft. They appeared to be human shapes charred horribly, as if by a great fire. He . . . estimated [their height] at between four and five feet tall, but [admitted that] it was just a guess on his part.

John asked Robert what [exactly] the photograph showed but was given no reply, and the photograph was returned to its place and the two went on to a game of chess. Not hearing from Robert for about a week, John decided to go to his house. . . . When he knocked on the door he was . . . confronted with an older woman who eyed him suspiciously. [When he asked for Robert,] the woman told him she was the only one living in the house, that she had lived there all her adult life, and had never seen or heard of anyone like his friend in the neighborhood. [She] asked John to go away, as she evidently thought he was crazy or out to do her harm.

John claimed that he never again saw Robert, though he received a birthday card from the man a few days later. He told Rick Hilberg that he was perplexed by the arrival of the card because he was certain he had never mentioned his birthday to Robert. In a personal note, Hilberg said he spoke with John on three or four subsequent occasions and always found him sincere and believable. John's story, Rick said, is "something I can't explain."

★　★　★

What to make of all of this? Some MIB experiences, such as PW's encounter with the men seeking tree samples and Jim Templeton's experience with the men in the black Jaguar, may well be the actions of tight-lipped government personnel. As for the other generally more outlandish episodes, if taken individually they could all be dismissed as hoax, fantasy, or overwrought imagination (and this includes my own recollection of the night in the mountains). Such skepticism is made more difficult, however, when one recognizes that many similar stories have come from widely separate locations. Furthermore, in at least some of these cases the aforementioned occult or religious component—the "dark man" association—remains clearly evident.

In January 1998, Scottish investigator Ron Halliday reported the experience of a UFO witness who, on the day of his sighting, saw twelve Men In Black enter a neighbor's house where "they disappeared into thin air." The witness described the clothing worn by the MIB as being similar to the garments worn by members of the clergy. Two individuals later turned up at the home of the witness to discuss the Bible and to tell him that the twelve men were the work of the Devil. "It wasn't the UFO that was this couple's concern," Halliday reflected, "but the MIB."[15]

Notes

1. The UFO flap of March 1966 was best known for the widely publicized sightings near Dexter and Hillsdale, Michigan. On March 14, wildly maneuvering UFOs were spotted during the early morning hours over three Michigan counties. On March 17, a huge flying disc approached a police patrol car near Milan, Michigan. The object came within twenty-five meters of the car, driven by a ten-year police veteran. On March 20, at about 10:00 P.M., a luminous object was observed hovering over a swamp near Dexter, Michigan, twelve miles from Ann Arbor, before darting away at high speed. More than fifty people, including police officers, watched the object. The following night in Hillsdale, twenty miles west of Dexter, more than eighty female students at the Hillsdale College, as well as the local Civil Defense director, watched a car-sized object maneuver over a swamp near the campus.

   Dr. J. Allen Hynek, a Northwestern University astronomer who at the time represented the Air Force as a special consultant, found himself in a room full of reporters and witnesses. One possible explanation for the wide range of sightings, he said, was "swamp gas"—methane from rotting marsh vegetation, which can spontaneously, and briefly, ignite and burn. The astronomer—miserable from a bone fracture resulting in a wired jaw and having alienated many locals due to what they perceived as snobbishness or arrogance on his part—emphasized that the explanation was at best partial and perhaps even entirely inadequate, but the press seized on the swamp gas comment and ignored everything else Hynek said that night. To further aggravate matters, the Air Force—looking for an easy fix—decided the swamp gas explanation was entirely appropriate for all sightings in the vicinity and classified the Michigan events as "explained." Until the time of his death in April 1986, Hynek was still trying to live down the experience.

2. The forest campsite was not completely invisible from the mountain road, but unless one knew exactly where to look it would have gone unnoticed, especially at night.

3. John A. Keel, *The Mothman Prophecies* (New York: Saturday Review Press, 1975; also Avondale Estates, Georgia, IllumiNet Press, 1991).

4. Ibid., pp. 55–57; also Gray Barker, *The Silver Bridge* (Clarksburg, West Virginia, Saucerian Books, 1970).

5. "Suddenly, The Bridge Just Wasn't There," *Patriot News,* Harrisburg, Pennsylvania, December 16, 1967, p. 1.

6. Keel, *The Mothman Prophecies,* pp. 11–14.

7. Gray Barker, *They Knew Too Much About Flying Saucers* (New York, University Books, 1956).

8. Eugene Steinberg, "The Caveat Emptor Interview: James W. Moseley," *Caveat Emptor,* No. 16, Winter 1988–89, pp. 7–14.
   The most notorious hoax perpetrated by Moseley and Gray Barker was "the Straith Letter." Using official State Department stationery, Barker drafted a letter from a mythical R. E. Straith representing an equally nonexistent "Cultural Exchange Committee." The letter was addressed to George Adamski, a well-known 1950s-era UFO "contactee," and posted by Moseley from a mailbox in Washington, D.C. The letter claimed to officially endorse Adamski's beliefs regarding visiting space aliens, and ultimately prompted an investigation by the FBI. Revealed as a hoax, the letter nonetheless wound up having "a life of its own," according to Moseley. Copies of the letter continued to surface through the years, notably during requests for UFO documents made via the Freedom of Information Act.

9. Gaelic folklore about the Banshee (a winged spirit whose wailing warns of death) probably grew out of stories about owls screaming at night. Owls can utter an astonishing assortment of nearly human screams and screeches, including a cry by the great-horned owl that sounds very much like a woman who is being strangled.

10. Pearl M. Nicholas, *The Valley Courier,* October 6, 1967, p. 1; also, Curt Sutherly, "The San Luis Valley Incident," *Official UFO,* August 1976, pp. 20–21, 45, 48.

11. Curt Sutherly, "Case History of a UFO Flap," *Official UFO*, December 1976, p. 41.

12. Andy Murray, "The Day the World Changed for the Templeton Family," *Courier*, Dumfries, Scotland, May 3, 1996; also, "Admit It, Someone, There Are UFOs About," *Westmoreland Gazette*, Kendal, England, October 4, 1996.

13. Rick R. Hilberg, *UFO Journal*, October 1981, pp. 5–7.

14. In a personal letter, Hilberg relates that his active involvement in ufology dates to late 1961, when he joined a group called the Cleveland Ufology Project. The project began about 1956 as an informal discussion group, with meetings conducted in the homes of participants. Hilberg became an officer of the group in early 1965. The following spring (1966) he and three others—Elmer Schutt, Ron Pelger, and Allan J. Manak—left to form a local chapter of the American UFO Committee.

    In November 1999, Hilberg's longtime friend and associate, Allan Manak, died following a prolonged illness. One of the more outspoken and influential members of the "Cleveland UFO crowd," Manak was an active writer and investigator of UFO and fortean phenomena until the time of his death. He was also a member of the permanent organizing committee of the National UFO Conference, which began in 1964 as the Congress of Scientific Ufologists.

15. Ron Halliday, "From the Shadows of UFOs Come MIBs," *Evening Times*, Glasgow, Scotland, January 31, 1998.

CHAPTER 4

The Invasion of
Boshkung Lake

IT BEGAN ON the evening of November 23, 1973.

Canadian realtors Earl Pitts and Jim Cooper were driving on Route 35 to their homes near Boshkung Lake in the town of Minden, Ontario. Suddenly an "awesome thing," as Pitts later described it, flashed through the sky from west to east and vanished from sight in seconds. The object, which the men estimated to be eighteen feet long, was "large in front and tapered" with a glowing front end and a white light at the tail.

Private pilot Dale Parnell of Stormy Lake, driving home that night with his wife, watched another (or perhaps the same) object pass nearby on Buckhorn Road. Pete Sawyer, of Hall's Lake, also spotted a strange flying object, though his sighting was during daylight hours. He told reporters that it looked like a helicopter without a tail. "It came down the gully by Shaws' heading for Boshkung Lake," he said. The top of the object was illuminated, the bottom half dark, and "that was the last I saw of it." Sawyer added that the object had four legs or landing gear that appeared to be partly raised.

Three months later, weird flying objects were still hanging around Boshkung Lake.[1] Mr. and Mrs. Ashley Lunham, residing in a lakeside house, told reporter Peter Courtney of the *Minden Progress* that strange aerial objects had scarcely missed a night since mid-November. The UFOs made no overt attempt to disturb residents or interfere with them, Mrs. Lunham said. But she did recall one rather disquieting incident.

The couple had just finished dinner one afternoon during mid-February 1974, when they saw a UFO move over the lake and turn toward their house. Midway across the lake the object began to glow with a brilliant white light as if generating excessive energy. The burst of power lasted for only a second or two, but in that brief interval the frost on the Lunhams' dining room windows melted! When Mrs. Lunham went to wipe up the water she discovered the glass was so hot "I couldn't touch it." The outside temperature at that time was twenty degrees below zero.

The Boshkung Lake UFOs arrived in assorted shapes and colors. Some objects were cigar-shaped and some were "polliwog" shaped. Some flashed amber, red, blue, or white lights. Others were rust brown or black in color, or sometimes a dull red. Each was reported to be carrying up to nine external "antennae," though they seemed to communicate, not by radio, but by flashing a kind of code back and forth with bright lights.

According to the Lunhams, flying objects appeared over the lake nearly every evening at sundown throughout the winter, arriving first singly or in pairs, then in greater numbers until the frozen lake surface was a virtual parking lot. The objects would then either settle to the surface, hang stationary over nearby power lines (a common UFO practice), or hover above holes in the ice that remained after ice fishermen had moved their huts. The UFO occupants, if there were any, were never seen.

After weeks of this nightly activity, the Lunhams decided to call the authorities. They may as well not have bothered. An officer of the Ontario Provincial Police arrived on the scene, pronounced the objects "reflections," and departed. After he had gone, the "reflections" shot straight up into the sky and streaked above the lake, their light reflected in its frozen surface.

The Lunhams next tried to interest the Canadian Department of National Defense. There they met with even less success.

On the morning of February 26, 1974, four UFOs were spotted within forty feet of the Lunham's home. These objects were of a different shape and design than any they'd seen before. Each had four wings, and an overall wingspan of about twenty feet. They were dark in color, and equipped with blue-white lights. Each, as it abruptly departed, discharged a fog.

Taken as a whole, the objects over Boshkung Lake were an unworldly conglomerate. They looked nothing at all like conventional aircraft. Their manner of flight was strange: takeoff was described as an upward bouncing motion not unlike a rubber ball. Sometimes when they launched they made an audible sound, a kind of dull "thumping" that faded as soon as the UFO was airborne. In flight horizontally, they moved erratically, and at greatly varying speeds.

Mrs. Lunham told reporters she didn't believe the objects were from outer space because they appeared almost every night for months. What's more, she said the UFO power plants didn't seem highly advanced—subject, evidently, to the same sort of problems as earthly engines: "Sometimes they start to fail . . ." She said a UFO experienced difficulty starting up the morning of Tuesday, February 26.

On Sunday, March 10, 1974, journalist Peter Courtney spotted a UFO over Boshkung Lake. The sighting—his first after a number of visits—was described in a *Minden Progress* article dated March 14.

In the article, Courtney acknowledged that one of his assignments was to cover the recurring UFO activity in Haliburton County, and in particular the Boshkung Lake area. After four trips he had collected numerous accounts, but he personally had observed nothing unusual. Then came the fifth visit. Wearing a snowmobile suit, and equipped with a 35mm camera and tripod for night photography, he arrived at the lake's east shore. The time, he reported in his article, was about 9:00 P.M. The weather was mild and the sky cloudless. The entire lake, he said, was "bathed in bright moonlight."

An hour passed and Courtney had about decided that this was to be another uneventful trip when "a dull red light" appeared on the far side of the lake. Moving above the treetops, the light traveled north in a slow, erratic manner before retracing its path and flying out of sight. The newsman had his camera ready, but the glowing red light proved too dull to photograph. Its movements, he wrote, were "too erratic" to be those of a regular aircraft, and he admitted that he was at a loss to explain away the object. He concluded that it "defied rational explanation."

While Courtney was quietly watching and puzzling over the strange flying light, others were preparing an ambush. That night more than fifty people gathered elsewhere along the lakeshore, determined to do something—anything—about the aerial interlopers. At about 10:00 P.M., the time of Courtney's sighting, members of a six-unit snowmobile squad took to the ice, firing high-powered rifles at the approaching UFOs. Mrs. Lunham told reporters that "a distant clunk" could be heard as bullets struck the exterior of the flying objects. Her reaction was nervousness and uneasiness. "I've had about as much of this as I can take," she said.

She wasn't the only resident fed up with the weird goings-on. Mrs. William Barnes, a housewife who—along with her husband—had watched UFOs near their home in Lochlin, Ontario, told reporters that a number of people had seen the objects and no one knew what to make of them. "We can't all be crazy," she observed.

One evening at the end of March 1974, Mr. and Mrs. Barnes watched a UFO maneuver about a half-mile from their house. Like many of the objects appearing over the lake, it sported red, white, and blue lights. Two nights later the same—or a very similar—

UFO returned to the exact location, but this time was joined by a second object. Mr. and Mrs. Barnes and a neighbor, Mrs. Lester Hicks, reported that the objects hovered for a time; then one of the two flew off rapidly. The second UFO departed more slowly, at a "cruising" speed, until it abruptly—and amazingly—dropped to the ground "out of sight!"

As the UFO sightings continued, residents of the area began finding what they believed were landing traces. Sometimes the trace was little more than a "depression" in the heavy lake ice. Other times it was significant, such as an odd pattern in the snow discovered by the Lunhams not far from their house. The unusual pattern was shown to *Lindsey* (Ontario) *Post* reporters, who described it in a March 14, 1974 story.

According to the *Post*, the pattern formed a "V-shape" in the snow combined with two "pad-like" markings. It was located within a copse of trees and was clearly visible despite erosion caused by the warm March sunshine. However, the pattern was only slightly odder than the location itself—within a wooded area. The *Post* observed that if the copse had sheltered a flying craft (and this was by no means certain), then the craft was either small enough to penetrate the forest canopy, or it had dropped to earth elsewhere and maneuvered to the location behind the Lunham house.

UFO activity at the lake continued well into April 1974. The final sighting of any consequence took place during the middle of the month, when Mrs. Wallace Brown of Lochlin looked out her bay window and observed an object with blue, green, and yellow lights moving erratically through the sky. Her television set became inoperative while the object was in the area. Neighbors also reported electromagnetic effects while the UFO was in the vicinity.

*   *   *

What all of this means is anyone's guess. However, as Mrs. Lunham observed, the objects at Boshkung Lake were probably not craft from outer space. Too many questions are raised by their long-term presence and activity—questions which fail to satisfy an extraterrestrial explanation.

If the objects were in fact spacecraft, they were powered by amazingly primitive engines—engines no better than terrestrial machines, starting with difficulty on cold winter mornings. Also, there is this business of objects dropping to the ground out of sight: vanishing, apparently, into the very earth. Finally, there are the sheer numbers of objects to be considered, and the fact that not once did anyone see occupants!

Mysterious, peculiar, and even a trifle absurd, the Boshkung Lake UFOs—like their innumerable counterparts observed around the world—appear destined to remain a mystery for a very long time to come.

Note

1. Curt Sutherly, "UFO Invasion of Boshkung Lake," November 1977, *FATE* magazine, pp. 55–58.

CHAPTER 5

In the Dark Sky

THE UFO "INVASION" at Boshkung Lake ended, and another year passed. It was October 1975, and I had reached a point in my life where—after a series of odd jobs and frustrated by a lack of direction—I found myself writing full time. The result was an outpouring of magazine articles on the strange and unknown, as well as stories of a more prosaic nature for regional radio and newspaper.

With my limited expertise, I knew that venturing into full-time writing was risky, but I had one thing in my favor: the pulp market for UFO, psychic, and fortean magazines was flourishing and—if the recent past was any indication—there appeared to be no shortage of subject material.[1]

Two and a half years earlier, in 1973, a series of UFO events had begun to unfold in the Pennsylvania countryside surrounding my home.[2] Within a matter of weeks a full-scale flap was underway, with reports occurring throughout the region. The flap persisted from spring into fall and ended just about the time events began at Boshkung Lake.

Along with the heavy UFO traffic, a phenomenon new to Pennsylvania occurred in 1973: livestock mutilations, also known as unexplained animal deaths (UADs). While not overtly connected to the UFO occurrences, there was a sense that the mutilations were a peripheral part of the ongoing events. They were, in any case, sufficiently frightening as to warrant concern.

The trauma inflicted during the UADs was of a form now widely recognized: surgically precise removal of bodily organs, and blood drained from the carcass with little or no loss on the ground. Livestock owners and lawmen who suspected Satanists or cultists, and who felt publicity would only encourage additional mayhem, quietly handled the UAD investigations. Dairy cattle seemed to be the main target, though there were reports of other animals being killed.

In March 1973, a farmer found a pair of sheep dead in an open pasture less than ten miles from my home. State police were notified and according to the investigating trooper (who spoke on the condition that I withhold the identity of the owner), the farmer claimed that the animals had been drained of blood. By the time police arrived, the owner—concerned about predators and disease—had already buried the carcasses. When I asked the trooper if he suspected the farmer had lied about the sheep or had exaggerated, perhaps for insurance reasons, he noted that it was possible but doubtful. He said the farmer had seemed genuinely unnerved and upset, as if the nature of the loss had been completely beyond his experience.

That same month near Pottstown, Pennsylvania, not far from Philadelphia, poultry and livestock fell prey to a mysterious, marauding beast. Descriptions varied, although witnesses agreed on two very bizarre points: the attacking creature had glowing (self-luminous) eyes and a sulfuric or rotten-egg stench. It was never killed, caught, or clearly identified despite nightly efforts by hunters and gun-toting vigilantes. The mayhem persisted for weeks, coinciding with abundant UFO activity.

Strange creature activity surfaced again in October 1973, this time in western Pennsylvania near the town of Greensburg.[3] As in

Pottstown, witnesses described something monstrous, something with glowing eyes and a stink of sulfur or rotten eggs. Much of the activity occurred at night, though several daytime sightings were made in wooded areas. The daylight witnesses—a female adult in one case and a number of frightened boys in two other cases—said they encountered large, ape-like hominids. State police found unusual tracks in the area where the boys had been playing. The tracks were large and three-toed. Specimens of tan-colored hair and abnormal fecal matter were also discovered at the scene.

UFO activity by this time was widespread throughout the state. In one instance in early November 1973, a large fireball flashed through the sky near my rented cottage. One of the witnesses was my aunt, Ethel Reed, who was passing by in her car. She said the object remained in view for about ten seconds and made no sound whatsoever. I was elsewhere when this occurred, interviewing four individuals who had had their own bizarre experience.

The four had been out spotlighting whitetail deer several nights earlier when they encountered a strange, brightly lit object. The incident occurred on November 4, 1973, in a forested area off Route 501 near Pine Grove, Pennsylvania. One of the witnesses said the object—a luminous floating orb—approached their parked vehicle. When the car spotlight was turned on the object, the light was reflected. "It acted like a mirror," the driver of the car said. "When we saw that, we figured we'd had enough and got out of there!"

By the end of 1973, UFO activity had stopped in the vicinity of my home even as events escalated elsewhere. The following autumn (1974) I found myself in northeastern Pennsylvania investigating an apparent UFO event in the town of Carbondale. This was followed by a period of comparative quiet that lasted until the fall of 1975.

* * *

The night of October 23, 1975 was cold and blustery and altogether too much like winter. In the living room of my little cottage, the "fireplace" window of the old gas furnace was venting jets of blue flame. Across the room, the television set babbled softly—barely audible over the noise arising from my manual typewriter. I was completing a news story on a routine township meeting, one of several such meetings I covered each month for the local paper. As I typed, the TV sound and picture was momentarily garbled by a citizen's band transmission from a passing vehicle. A single, understandable expression escaped the mix of signals. The term was "U-foe," or UFO.

A minute later, the telephone rang. I glanced at my watch: it was 9:35 P.M. The caller was the night shift police reporter for the *Lebanon Daily News*. The man sounded excited, which he seldom was—he'd been a cop reporter too long. He told me that he'd just gotten a call about a strange object flying over the city.

Explaining, the night man said his call had come from an off-duty Civil Defense dispatcher, and that according to the dispatcher, CD personnel were being flooded with inquiries about a silent, blimp-like object. Police too were being swamped with calls. Faced with an already heavy workload, the night reporter found himself unable to pursue the lead and decided to telephone me. I thanked him and hung up, thinking about synchronicity and a story published in the afternoon paper.

The story (which I had written) was an interview with Lucius Farish, a UFO historian in Arkansas who had written a number of carefully researched articles about the little known "phantom airship" flap of 1896–97. The early flap involved cigar-shaped objects observed at intervals years before the development of reliable dirigible aircraft.[4] Mulling over the interview, I wondered whether its publication might have somehow triggered the immediate UFO event. Then I dismissed the idea and began making telephone calls.

An hour later, I had compiled sufficient information for a short news story that I hoped would be useful to Rob McNamee, the city editor. I had no way of knowing that my story would be greatly expanded, or that it would serve as the basis for a front page headline report.

* * *

As it turned out, John (Jack) Lindermuth, a former Korean War correspondent and wire editor for the *Daily News*, was among those who saw the UFO. When he arrived at work at his customary early starting time, he discovered my story on McNamee's desk. After inserting his own observations into the article, he began making phone inquiries. Hours later the front page of the day's edition proclaimed: MYSTERY AIRCRAFT SPURS SPECULATION ABOUT UFOS, while the lead told readers, "Whatever else it may have been, it wasn't one of the Goodyear blimps."

Lindermuth, who at the time owned a house a couple of miles north of the city, saw the UFO as he stepped outside at approximately 9:40 P.M. Illuminated by white lights, he said the northbound object appeared to be in "the configuration of a blimp when first sighted. However, as the object passed directly overhead, the lights depicted more the shape of a horseshoe crab." The object, Lindermuth said, made no audible sound.

Lindermuth's inquiries the next morning included calls to local Army helicopter personnel, who denied any knowledge of the occurrence. He also called the Goodyear Tire and Rubber Company in Akron, Ohio, and eventually spoke with Tom Reilly, a public relations director for Goodyear's blimp division. According to Reilly: "None of our blimps was in your area last night." Explaining, Reilly said the airship *Mayflower* was in Alabama at the time; the *America* in Elkhart, Indiana, and the *Columbia* in California where it was permanently based.

Reilly's comments, along with those from the Army, were added to the story and the result was a solid, credible news report. The afternoon edition hit the streets and other witnesses came forward, including a patrolman for the North Cornwall/West Lebanon township police department.

The patrolman, Donald Wengert, said he was in his parked cruiser just west of the city when the object passed overhead. He described "four burning lights in a flattened half-moon shape with a fifth [light] top center." He estimated the altitude at about 200 to 300 feet. He said the object flew "too fast for a hot air balloon and too slow for a jet plane," but he was equally certain that it wasn't a helicopter or a prop-driven airplane.

The following night, October 24, more "dirigible" sightings occurred. On the third night, events escalated dramatically.

★　★　★

In 1975, at the time of the Lebanon County airship sightings, public opinion about UFOs in the United States was perhaps best defined as confused. The government, then as now, denied interest in the subject. The Air Force was officially out of the picture—its investigative unit-cum-public relations front, Project Blue Book, long since closed. The media, after a prolonged period of routinely downplaying sightings and ridiculing witnesses, was suddenly attempting to demonstrate—as one wag put it—"a renewed and sincere interest" in the UFO phenomenon. The result, overall, was mixed signals to the masses.

Around this same time a change was occurring within the civilian research community. Competitive and quarrelsome by nature, UFO investigators were squabbling more than ever before. Arguments erupted over the nature of the phenomenon and how best to study it, and competing egos clashed, but the root problem was simply that—after nearly three decades of documented "flying saucer" activity—ufologists had finally recognized that a large segment of the public regarded ufology as more of a cult than a science. To dispel this view, UFO investigators realized that they needed to act professionally in spite of conflicting views, or to at least offer a professional front. Unfortunately, every attempt to do so only seemed to escalate the unremitting war of words.

To make matters worse, only a handful of professional or even amateur scientists were, by 1975, enrolled in any serious study of the phenomenon. As a result, the scientific method was rarely employed. Field investigations usually fell to journalists or lay researchers armed only with a notebook or a tape recorder. High-tech tools were in short supply: there were no hand-held video cameras—only cumbersome film cameras and that favorite of sports photographers, the 35mm camera with high-speed motor drive; there were no cellular phones, no powerful home computers for cataloging and comparing reports, and of course no access to a World Wide Web. But if cell phones and personal computers were nonexistent, nearly everyone had a citizens band radio either at home or in the car.

* * *

At approximately 9:00 P.M. on October 25, 1975, two men were raking and burning leaves behind the Woods Creek sporting goods store in northern Lebanon County when a dark shape, punctuated by white lights, soared overhead. During an interview the following day, one of the men said he at first thought the lights were stars showing through a break in the cloud cover (the night was overcast), but then he saw the silhouette of the object and realized his mistake. As the men gaped in astonishment, the UFO gained altitude and settled into a stationary position over the nearby Blue Mountain.

Others in the area soon spotted the object, and a CB radio alert went out. It wasn't long before sightseers began to gather. Local authorities—including members of the county sheriff's department, civil defense, and state police—also heard the call and responded; but by the time they too arrived the object was visible only as a solitary bright light over the mountaintop.

At the same time, deep in the mountain, a group of raccoon hunters was on its way to the summit. They had entered Blue Mountain from the western end of a somewhat remote, low-lying area known as Swope Valley, at a point about two and a half miles north of the mountaintop. The elevation at the summit is 1400 feet, with the Appalachian Trail following the ridge at that location. The terrain on the mountain is rough and makes a difficult climb under the best of circumstances.

The hunters were nearing the summit when they heard a series of eerie sounds, like "tearing metal." Unaware of the nearby UFO activity, their immediate reaction was that an airplane had crashed on the mountaintop. Visibility was limited, not only by darkness but by an odd, heavy fog descending on the slopes. The hunters became disoriented and as they stumbled along began to realize that the strange sounds were not subsiding and if anything were growing more distinct and ever more frightening. Clearly, the noise was not from an aircraft, crashed or otherwise, and in fact they had no idea what it was or meant. To them, it sounded like the gates of Hell were opening up.

Panicked, the hunters fled, and at 11:00 P.M. they exited the mountain five miles from their point of entry, not far from the Woods Creek store. They saw lights burning inside and a short while later—pale with fright—were frantically relating their experience to the owner of the store.

★　★　★

During a series of interviews the following day, I pieced together the events of the previous night. Many years later, while reviewing old files in preparation for this book, I was struck by the similarity of the strange sounds on Blue Mountain to those reported during an even earlier set of events occurring some two and one-half years earlier.

In April 1973, in the mountains of Colorado, several individuals were camping in a cabin at the foot of Mt. Blanca, the tallest peak in the Sangre de Christo mountain range. The group included a deputy sheriff from Colorado, two men from Texas, and Floyd Murray, a fortean researcher from Folsom, Pennsylvania. The cabin was owned by a man who had permanent residence near Alamosa in the San Luis Valley.[5]

According to Murray, the campers—who were there specifically to investigate ongoing UFO and fortean phenomena—were awakened late one night by a horrible screeching, as if someone or something incredibly strong was shredding metal. The noise eventually ceased only to be replaced by a heavy crashing, like the sound of a large animal pounding through the brush. Murray said he'd almost desperately wanted to go outside to try and locate the source of the noise, but everyone else—including the deputy, who was armed with both a rifle and a revolver—sensibly declined.[6]

The following morning the members of the expedition left the cabin and began a search of the vicinity. They discovered large tracks leading away through the snow: "Three-toed footprints," Murray said, "like the ones reported at other places where fortean events occur." The men followed the tracks for about half a mile through the snow and mud before the trail faded completely in wet ground. Murray said that although the tracks were three-toed, there was absolutely no doubt that they were bipedal—made by an animal walking on two legs. The tracks measured about ten and a half inches long and six inches wide. The deputy sheriff, who had spent twenty years hunting in the Colorado mountains, remarked that it was the first time he ever saw anything like them—though this was not so for other members of the expedition!

In May 1971, the two from Texas, along with a man from Arkansas, were camping in the same cabin at the base of Mt. Blanca. During the early morning of May 24 they were disturbed by "assorted unexplained noises," followed by the appearance of an odd shaft of light and a "shadowy figure" on the patio outside the window. According to a detailed report on the incident, a copy of which was given to Floyd Murray: "Around 3:00 A.M. all hell broke loose behind the cabin . . . Thrashings and crashing were heard" and something took hold of the back door "and shook it violently . . . as though trying to tear it off its hinges." Inside the cabin pandemonium erupted, but by the time the campers reached the back door "utter silence prevailed." Outside, they discovered a series of "apparent footprints." Years later, Murray told me that the tracks discovered in 1973 were identical to those reported by the 1971 expedition.

* * *

The events of October 25, 1975, near the Woods Creek store at Blue Mountain, marked the final appearance of the phantom airship in Lebanon County. But this was not quite the end of that particular flap.

Shortly before midnight on October 30, I received a phone call from a man who spoke excitedly about seeing a UFO. I'll refer to him only by first name: John. I had known him since boyhood. His older brother, Joseph, was a friend and a member of my high-school graduating class. Both brothers possessed a strong sense of humor, and I frankly suspected the call was a prank.

John related that at about 10:15 P.M., he and two other men had been in a vehicle traversing Little Mountain in northern Lebanon County when they were confronted with a spherical object that crossed ahead of them in the dark sky. The object, moving east to west, was luminous white with "rods" or "projections" extending from the bottom. John said the UFO appeared to be quite large, though its size could not be gauged accurately. The object was quickly lost to view behind a screen of trees.

John included one other detail, and when I heard it I was suddenly less skeptical about his story. He said the object "bounced" through the air much as a rubber ball bounces along the ground. This is not a commonly reported UFO characteristic, though it was identical to the "take-off" motion reported in UFOs at Boshkung Lake. Recognizing this, I also realized that the "rods" or "projections" described by John sounded suspiciously like the "antennae" reported on many of the Boshkung Lake objects. The problem was that in late 1975 only a handful of people in the United States were at all aware of the eighteen-month-old events in Ontario, and even fewer knew the significant details. John would not have had that information, which—to me at least—made his story far more plausible.

* * *

On October 31, 1975, the *Lebanon Daily News* carried a front-page update—by Jack Lindermuth and myself—on the UFO activity. Included was the following account:

> On the night of the original sightings, October 23, a resident of a trailer park in North Lebanon Township observed a different type of aerial phenomenon. The witness, who has asked to remain anonymous, said he was returning from Lebanon and was about to enter his trailer when he spotted two helicopters hovering at a low altitude over an adjacent cornfield.
>
> His curiosity was aroused by the "copters" seemingly aimless activity of passing back and forth over the field. His immediate assumption was that the ships were state police helicopters involved in some phase of a drug raid or in a search for escaped convicts. The helicopters were illuminated by the lights from the trailer court and he said they appeared to be grayish.
>
> Obtaining a pair of binoculars from his car, he took a closer look at the helicopters and said he could see no markings of any kind on the ships. Perplexed, he watched for several minutes until the ships flew away.
>
> Sightings of similar unmarked helicopters have become a peripheral phase in the UFO puzzle in many parts of the world in recent years. However, our informant was unaware of this and his story was only revealed when he questioned a *Daily News* report that there was no military aviation activity the night of the UFO sightings. The man was also not aware of the UFO sightings when he first observed the helicopters at approximately 11:00 P.M., on October 23.

Another couple residing at the same trailer park reported that on the following evening they saw a small globular light fly a zigzag pattern horizontally across the same cornfield several times and then disappear.

        ★ ★ ★

On Halloween night, October 31, I drove my car across the Little Mountain, following the route that John said he had traveled on the previous evening. The weather was cold and extremely clear—an exhilarating night with a bright panorama of stars. Traversing Little Mountain, I turned west through picturesque Monroe Valley at the foot of the Appalachians. I was nearing the western edge of the valley when something to the north caught my eye.

Pulling the car to the side of the road, I grabbed my binoculars and stepped into the night air. Off in the distance a white light was moving aimlessly, erratically back and forth, up and down. I focused with the binoculars but was unable to make out details—only a nondescript ball of yellowish-white light. I watched for several minutes before the light abruptly vanished, then waited for several more. The light failed to reappear. Shivering from more than the cold, I climbed back into the car and drove home.

Notes

1. A large number of pulp newsstand magazines flourished briefly during the 1970s as publishers tried to cash in on the growing interest in UFO and paranormal phenomena. A partial magazine list includes such titles as *Argosy UFO, Beyond Reality, Cosmic Frontiers, Occult, Official UFO, Probe the Unknown, Psychic World,* and *UFO Report*—the last a quarterly magazine published by the editors of *Saga* (a well-known men's magazine of the period) and far and away the best of the bunch. Many of today's best-known UFO researchers and writers had their start in these magazines. As an example, in two issues of *Official UFO*—taken at random from my collection of yellowing old magazines—I found articles by Jerome Clark, Kevin Randle, Lucius Farish, Don Berliner, Jenny Randles, Richard Hall, and Don Worley—all now widely recognized as experts in the field.

2. Curt Sutherly, "1973: Madness in the Keystone State," *Official UFO*, April 1976, pp. 20-21, 52–53.

3. Allen V. Noe, "ABSMAL Affairs in Pennsylvania and Elsewhere," *Pursuit*, October 1973 (Vol. 6, No. 4), pp. 84–89.

4. Although a number of crude dirigibles were tested in Europe as early as 1852, it wasn't until July 2, 1900 that an extended flight was made in a craft piloted by Count Ferdinand von Zeppelin, whose name would become synonymous with dirigible aeronautics. Zeppelin's flight lasted twenty minutes. On September 10, 1907, the British Army tested an airship carrying three occupants, and in April 1917 the U.S. Navy followed with three successful flights at Pensacola, Florida. After the third flight the Navy dirigible was damaged and never repaired.

   Phantom airship activity occurred in Europe in 1892, and in the United States (California) in 1896. The following year additional sightings occurred in Nebraska, Kansas, Iowa, Michigan, and numerous other states. By April 1897 newspapers throughout the country were reporting airship activity. Many of the published accounts were later proven to be fictitious, though at least some of the initial sightings were clearly authentic.

5. Colorado's San Luis Valley has a history of inexplicable occurrences dating to precolonial times. UFOs, strange creatures, and unexplained animal deaths are some of the phenomena frequently reported in the valley. An excellent first-person chronicle of the region's unusual history is Christopher O'Brien's *The Mysterious Valley* (St. Martin's Press, 1996).

6. Personal communications with Floyd Murray during late 1988 and early 1989.

part two

To the End of the Millennium

Controversial subjects generate polarized responses.

Christopher O'Brien
The Mysterious Valley

CHAPTER 6

Black Squares and Electric Railroad Lanterns

THE COLD WAS numbing, the temperature near zero, when the "thing" arrived and buried itself in the mud and silt at the bottom of William McCarthy's farm pond. The event rippled through the sleepy town of Wakefield (pop. 1,400), interrupting a New Year that, although cold and snowy, was otherwise unremarkable.

Located in southeast New Hampshire not far from the Maine border, Wakefield was understandably unprepared for its mysterious visitor. The day was January 10, 1977. Twenty-six-year-old Thomas McCarthy found himself out in the cold, staring at the frozen surface of his father's pond where something very odd was occurring. The entire pond was beginning to melt and "it was five degrees above zero" with a blizzard in progress, he later explained.

Startled and a bit shaken, Thomas alerted his parents, William and Dorothy, to the melting ice. They soon found that the one-hundred-foot-long pond contained a hole in the frozen surface some three feet in diameter and perfectly round. What's more, "a black square object" could be seen through the hole, settling into the pond bottom.[1]

The strange black object had penetrated ice that was eighteen inches thick, William McCarthy later told reporters. He said he had no "logical explanation" for what had occurred except that perhaps a piece of space hardware from a "disintegrating space capsule or booster" had struck his pond.

*   *   *

McCarthy, fifty-two, a professional breeder of saddle horses, gave a more detailed account of his observations to UFO researcher Betty Hill of Portsmouth, New Hampshire. Hill passed along the information in a letter dated January 29, 1977. She wrote: "McCarthy told me that he found the eighteen inch-thick ice melting, and it continued to melt while he watched. He looked down into the hole and saw a twelve-inch-square black object, which was also seen by two other family members [wife Dorothy and son Thomas]."

Curiosity overwhelming his better judgment, McCarthy decided to try to retrieve the object. "He went to the barn for a hoe, rake, and a long stick." Using the stick as a probe, McCarthy discovered "that the object had apparently settled into the mud at the bottom of the pond, for he found a three-foot hole [in the mud] the same shape as the object." By now, according to Hill, McCarthy had begun to feel "very uncomfortable" due to the storm and extremely cold temperature.

Returning to the house, McCarthy notified a friend who in turn contacted police. The call for assistance, as it turned out, proved to be about the same as opening a Pandora's Box.

Two police officers arrived soon thereafter with a Geiger counter and checked the pond for radiation. According to Betty Hill, they got a reading of about four roentgens—high enough to be considered potentially dangerous and prompting a warning that the family should not allow the horses to drink from the pond. (For purposes of comparison, radioactive fallout from a distant nuclear test is usually measured in thousandths of a roentgen.) Soon Civil Defense personnel arrived and took additional readings. In a statement to reporters, George McAvoy, then director of Civil Defense for New Hampshire observed: "It's not a hoax. There was some phenomenon."

CD Deputy Director Wesley Williams, who took the first Civil Defense readings, told the media that three different counters showed three different readings. One Geiger counter read zero, one low, and one about three roentgens per hour. Williams said that when he arrived the pond ice was still melting, so he was forced to take his readings at a distance of several yards from a marker indicating the original three-foot hole. He noted that he was in over his boots while still ten feet from the marker. The instrument that gave a high reading was later returned to a Civil Defense laboratory for suspected equipment failure. According to George McAvoy, no amount of testing revealed any fault with the counter. Subsequent testing of the other two instruments also uncovered no problem.

Twelve hours after the first readings were taken, Geiger counters showed negative radioactivity around the pond. However, federal officials (Energy Research and Development Administration, Washington, D.C.) speculated that if an object had indeed settled to the bottom, the combination of water, ice, and mud might have blocked further radiation emissions, making them undetectable.

★ ★ ★

In the days following the arrival of the "thing," as it came to be known, the Wakefield Pandora's Box opened still further, allowing the demons of bureaucracy to spill out onto the countryside.

On Thursday, January 13, 1977, state officials arrived, examined the pond, and decided there was nothing hidden beneath the ice and mud. Included in this task force were members of the National Guard, representatives of the New Hampshire Disaster

Office, assorted health officials, and individuals from the state's Criminal Division. The task force placed the area under tight security, and everyone in town was told not to talk about the thing that wasn't there.

Meanwhile, a representative for the office of New Hampshire Governor Meldrim Thomson, Jr. was explaining how "the entire report is false; [there is] no evidence of any foreign object in the small pond." At about the same time, WBZ-TV in Boston was airing a film clip showing a basketball-sized mass being removed from the pond (later said to have been mud and silt samples from the pond floor). As if this weren't enough, Colonel Leon Parker of the state adjutant's office put his foot in his mouth when he contradicted Governor Thomson: "We know some object dropped into the farmer's pond," he stated publicly.

In Washington, D.C., a Pentagon spokesman told reporters that officials with the New Hampshire National Guard were asking if the object was a fallen artificial satellite. The Guard had inquired with the North American Air Defense Command (ADC), but according to the spokesman, an ADC check showed no evidence that a satellite—or any part of one—had fallen on Wakefield.

In Wakefield itself, speculation abounded despite the official "gag order." According to William McCarthy, the attitude in the town was that if you were not supposed to talk about it, then "there must be something to it." The farmer admitted to reporters that he had been swamped with telephone calls from excited individuals: "What color are the spaceships?" one caller asked. McCarthy, calm despite the unrest around him, said such calls were an exaggeration. There were no "little green men," he said, and no "flashing lights," and no "thunder."

Meanwhile, the Wakefield "thing" was news even in Canada. On January 13, the same day that state officials arrived in Wakefield, television stations in Ontario reported that an odd tremor had rattled the town of Cobourg (pop. 11,000). What made the tremor unusual, the media reported, was that it not only happened just before the "crash" in Wakefield, but it also failed to register on seismic instruments.

Some observers noted that Cobourg is only a few miles from Port Hope, Ontario, where nuclear research was being conducted. That Cobourg should be shaken as Wakefield received a radioactive object from the sky seemed like an extremely odd coincidence. Furthermore, Wakefield and Cobourg are not far apart geographically—separated in a straight line by no more than four hundred miles. Still, it is unlikely that the Wakefield object was linked in any way to research at Port Hope. On the other hand, it is possible that the shockwave felt in Cobourg was caused by the object, which may have been moving faster than sound before hitting the pond. The object would have left an audible track (a sonic boom) along a path that carried it over Cobourg. This, however, raises another question: why was there no shockwave or audible disturbance at the point of impact? One answer is that the object, device, whatever it was (and keep in mind its reported shape), slowed down before hitting the pond! It came in under controlled flight!

★　★　★

Strange objects have a way of falling into small lakes and ponds. Three years earlier, on November 9, 1974, in the town of Carbondale, Pennsylvania, a "mysterious glowing object" plunged into a small silt pond on the outskirts of the town. There as in Wakefield, officials insisted that the affair was nothing more than a hoax.

The Carbondale "fireball," as it came to be known, was observed at about 7:00 P.M. on November 9 by three teenage boys: Bill Lloyd, his younger brother, John, and a friend, Bob Gillette. The boys told Carbondale police that when they first saw the object, it looked like a red fireball. They said it approached from the east, crossed over nearby Salem Mountain and then hovered! An instant later it plunged into the pond. According to the three youngsters, the UFO "turned the color of a bright star" while it hovered. Police

UFO investigators gather in Lima, Ohio, in 1978. From left, John Timmerman, treasurer of the Center for UFO Studies, Rick Hilberg, and the late Dr. J. Allen Hynek. (Photo by Carol Hilberg)

later admitted they received at least one earlier phone call about a UFO.

Within the hour other calls came into police headquarters. Finally, around 9:00 P.M., officers John Barbaro and Joseph Jacobina were dispatched to the pond where they reported seeing a "glowing object" about twenty feet out in the water. Shortly thereafter, acting police chief Francis Dottle was notified; he dispatched twelve additional (regular and special) police to the scene. Officers also arrived from nearby Forest City, and from Greenfield and Fell townships. At one point, officer Jacobina discharged his service revolver into the water, and according to Bob Gillette the glow "moved." No further action was taken until after midnight, when firefighters arrived from a nearby community armed with a huge net.

According to a report published in the *Scranton* (Pennsylvania) *Times*, the scene around the pond took on "the look of a science fiction thriller as the net was hooked around the object."[2] This was at about 2:45 A.M. As the firefighters hauled on the net, the glowing object slipped free and settled into the silt at the bottom of the pond. Later the glow vanished and police surmised that the object had become buried under the silt. No additional attempts to raise the light were made that night.

Sunday, November 10, two professors from Philadelphia's Temple University arrived and asked permission to don scuba gear and search the pond bottom. The two were Dr. Laurence Berry, a psychologist, and George Kelly, a meteorology instructor. However, Chief Dottle would not allow the men to dive. Next, police contacted Dr. J. Allen Hynek, then head of the Center for UFO Studies in Illinois. Hynek informed police that a UFO investigator from Port Crane, New York, would be dispatched to act as an advisor. Events as they occurred from this point on are unclear—the details mired in confusion and obscurity.

★ ★ ★

In 1974, at the time of the Carbondale occurrence, I was just beginning to place a real emphasis on my writing. Up until then I had been penning occasional news copy and magazine articles while holding down various full-time jobs. Now, I was expanding my part-time effort to include serving as a regular correspondent for the *Lebanon Daily News*, some three hours drive time from Carbondale. Because I had a day off from my full-time job, I was able to convince city editor Rob McNamee to assign me to the "fireball" story. However, by the time I arrived in Carbondale, on Monday, November 11, the entire episode had been branded a hoax, with the Lloyd brothers and Gillette made to look like pranksters.

Checking in with police, I found myself in the office of acting Chief Dottle. When I explained my presence, the man stared at me. "Not another one!" he barked. "This town's been crawling with reporters." A silence followed as I pondered the unexpected outburst. Dottle himself broke the silence as he reached behind his desk and produced a silvery object, which he waved in the air. "This is your UFO!" he declared. It was an electric railroad lantern.

Surprised, but suspicious, I continued to press for details about the events of the two previous days. According to Dottle, the lantern had been retrieved from the pond (by a scuba diver, I later learned) still glowing, yet it appeared undamaged by roughly nine hours of immersion in water, and its batteries had apparently operated the entire time without fading. My effort to elicit more information about this amazing lantern only resulted in terse, impatient comments from Dottle. However, the chief did manage to make one point especially clear: he wanted me to leave Carbondale immediately. The man was clearly frustrated and showing evident stress. Nonetheless, I had to suppress a smile as his reaction brought to mind all the old western films I'd ever seen in which the sheriff ordered the stranger out of town.

Of course I didn't leave right off. Instead, I spoke with people on the streets and in various places of business, trying to make sense of what had transpired during the hours I had been en route. Public attitude was about the same as in Wakefield. Many were convinced that something unknown had fallen into the pond—that the electric lantern was merely a device of convenience, and that local police were reciting a script prepared by higher authority. There was even an unconfirmed report that an object had been taken from the pond, loaded into an unmarked van and driven away.

★   ★   ★

Putting aside any and all speculation about origin, as well as the usual "official" pronouncements that there is never anything to it, the fact remains that mysterious objects do drop from the skies, and not always with quiet consideration. On occasion, these aerial visitors raise pure hell.

Such an event occurred at Upper Scott Lake near Pullman, Michigan, just fifteen minutes after the year 1970 began. The lake, located on a YMCA camp ground, was under the supervision of Mr. and Mrs. James Eastep, who were in the camp house playing cards with relatives at the time of the incident.

Suddenly the building shook violently, nearly tossing the card players to the floor. Storm windows blew out of the walls. A mile and a half away, in Pullman, shockwaves were felt. Even more astonishing were subsequent reports from the town of Bravo, four miles to the north, where books were thrown from shelves and windows rattled.

Later in the day, Jim Eastep discovered additional damage to the camp. In the dining lodge, picture windows were shattered. So were small windowpanes and a light fixture, and even the fireplace frame. Wooden window shutters on several cabins also showed heavy damage, looking as if "an ax had cut them to ribbons."

When he searched beyond the buildings, Eastep discovered a huge hole—forty feet across—in the icy lake surface. The hole was about two hundred yards from shore. Ice chunks were scattered as much as one hundred feet from the hole, which appeared to be the point of impact of something from above.

Sheriff's deputies called to the scene decided that, probably because it was New Year's Day, somebody had been playing with dynamite. Persons experienced in the use of heavy explosives were quick to ridicule this theory, noting that an incredible amount of TNT would be needed to cause such extensive damage (not to mention sending the shockwaves four miles into Bravo). Eastep himself said that he had witnessed a truck load of dynamite explode in Korea in the same type of weather, and the dynamite explosion caused less noise and shock.

Still other puzzling factors came to light. One resident claimed that just before the explosion he heard the sound of an aircraft passing over the camp. Another individual said the needle of her home barometer started whirling prior to the blast. Moreover, there was the strange mound of mud found by Eastep and his brother-in-law, Dale Lamb. This mound, containing seaweed from the lakebed, had oozed upward through a three-foot hole in the ice about thirty-five feet from shore, forming a bulge two feet high. By afternoon on New Year's Day the mound had receded. Clearly something struck the lake; something with highly unusual and potentially deadly properties.

★ ★ ★

On January 16, 1977, the *Boston Globe* published an editorial titled "The Wakefield Monster," which effectively summarized both private and official attitudes regarding events in that town. In part, it appeared as follows (reprinted courtesy of the *Boston Globe*):

> Four days of speculation, inspection, tests and jabs at the pond have left the tiny town on the Maine border with little more than an argument over whether anything out of the ordinary ever happened at all.
>
> Witnesses to the "alleged" event, as newspapers are calling the activity, claim that on Monday a 3-foot-wide hole appeared in the 18-inch-thick ice on a farm pond owned by Mr. and Mrs. William McCarthy. Ice around the hole melted, a flat, black object was seen nestled in the mud, more holes developed, and the Wakefield police were summoned.
>
> Wild radioactivity levels were recorded at the site, security was thrown up around the farm, and the New Hampshire National Guard was ordered to search the suspect pond. Spectators at that operation reported that the guardsmen chopped out a big chunk of ice, raised the alleged object and dispatched it to Concord.
>
> There Gov. Meldrim Thomson, Jr., whose response to all of this has included ingeniously ordering the 1,400-odd townspeople into silence, announced after the probe-and-remove mission that nothing had been found and that the alleged mystery was officially over.

*   *   *

Over for whom? For those who may have found something in the pond, doubtlessly! But for the people of Wakefield, and for those who followed the matter from afar with great interest, the mystery—after all these years—remains far from finished.

Are we being protected from some knowledge that military and political leaders feel could cause us harm? Or are we being shielded from the fear they themselves know every time they deal with the unknown?

Notes

1. Curt Sutherly, "Inside Story of the New Hampshire UFO Crash," *UFO Report*, July 1977, pp. 22, 60–61, 63–64.

2. Bill Halpin, "An Eerie Glow Fills Pond," *Scranton Times*, Nov. 11, 1974.

CHAPTER 7

The Disinformation Game

THERE ARE THOSE who believe the United States government, quite literally, has the answer to the UFO puzzle. They claim that on a stormy night in July 1947, an alien spacecraft crashed in an arid region of New Mexico, and that military personnel retrieved both wreckage and the bodies of the dead crew members.

The story is an old one, circulating for forty years as nothing more than a rumor. In 1987 a new twist was added: a mysterious document that stated the crash had prompted a top-secret government operation. At last, there seemed to be proof.

A storm of controversy quickly ensued. Accusations and demands were rife within UFO research groups. The debate found its way into print and even onto television. UFO buffs everywhere came to know the code name for the government operation supposedly behind it all: "Majestic 12" or MJ-12.

In mid-1989 I was asked to write a magazine article examining the validity of the MJ-12 document.[1] The editor wanted a comprehensive piece—an article that would include everything then

91

known on the subject. Not long after I received a copy of the MJ-12 document from researcher Floyd Murray, who also sent photocopies of related papers and articles, and on request obtained necessary telephone numbers. Sifting through the material took weeks. More time was spent interviewing various persons. Eventually the article was completed.

In the process, I learned that the MJ-12 papers first surfaced in December 1984, when they were sent on undeveloped 35mm film to Jaime Shandera, a Los Angeles-based documentary film producer. Shandera and two associates, Stanton T. Friedman and William L. Moore, both well-known in UFO research circles, withheld the document until May 1987, ostensibly to try to determine its validity before releasing it to a wider audience.

At the heart of the MJ-12 papers is the legend of the "crashed alien spaceship." Briefly, the story is this: in early July 1947, a public relations officer at Roswell Army Air Base, New Mexico, issued a statement which said, in part: "the intelligence office of the 509th [Atomic] Bomb Group of the Eighth Air Force, Roswell Army Air Base, was fortunate enough to gain possession of a [flying] disc through the cooperation of one of the local ranchers and the Sheriffs office of Chaves County. . . . Action was immediately taken and the disc was picked up at the rancher's home. It was inspected at the Roswell Army Air Field and subsequently loaned by Major [Jesse] Marcel [the intelligence officer in charge of the retrieval operation] to higher headquarters."

Almost immediately, higher headquarters recanted the story. Instead of a flying disc, the object was said to be the "wreckage of a high altitude weather observation device" consisting of a "box-kite and a balloon," along with a "star-shaped tinfoil target to reflect radar." The balloon explanation was attributed to Army Brigadier General Roger M. Ramey, commander of the Eighth Air Force at Fort Worth.[2] Ramey's explanation notwithstanding, the rumor persisted that the object really was a flying disc. Forty years later, the MJ-12 papers seemed to verify the story of a crashed alien craft.

Dated November 18, 1952, the MJ-12 document appears to be a briefing written by Rear Admiral R. H. Hillenkoetter for President-elect Dwight D. Eisenhower. Also included is a purported memorandum, dated September 24, 1947, signed by President Harry Truman to Defense Secretary James Forrestal, calling for the creation of "Operation Majestic 12."

Majestic 12, according to page two of the briefing document, is "a Top Secret Research and Development/Intelligence operation responsible only to the President of the United States." This alleged operation is carried out at the direction of twelve highly placed individuals having a combined military/civilian background—hence the code name.

"On 07 July, 1947," the document continues, "a secret operation was begun to assure recovery of the wreckage of this object for scientific study." It goes on to state that "four small human-like beings had apparently ejected from the craft at some point before it exploded." The bodies were found some "two miles east of the wreckage site. All four were dead and badly decomposed due to action by predators and exposure to the elements during the approximately one-week time period which had elapsed before their discovery."

I've discussed this matter with naturalists having a working knowledge of animal decomposition, with a veterinarian, and with a coroner of many years experience. All have rendered essentially the same opinion: a body—human or animal—would not "badly decompose" in a hot, dry region. Instead, the arid desert environment would dehydrate the carcass, resulting in a kind of mummification. Furthermore, the coroner with whom I spoke noted that if predators or scavengers had attacked the carcasses, they would, after a week, have reduced the bodies to bones. In short, there is a great deal to suspect about this part of the MJ-12 document. What, then, of the rest of the document?

★ ★ ★

When the MJ-12 papers first came to light, two researchers in particular were immediately at odds over whether or not the document is genuine. One was Philip J. Klass, the other Stanton Friedman. Neither man is exactly what one might call a dunderhead.

Klass, of Washington, D.C., is an aviation expert and a contributing editor for a leading aviation magazine. He is ufology's best-known (and, for some, most despised) skeptical investigator, and like many others is convinced the MJ-12 papers are a hoax.

Friedman, on the other hand, was at one point quite vocal in his defense of the purported document. His background is that of nuclear physicist and UFO lecturer. He has worked on numerous classified government projects, including programs to develop nuclear powered aircraft and nuclear-thrust rockets.[3] He lives in New Brunswick, Canada.

For a long time the debate between the two men was more or less tit for tat—that is, fairly well balanced, without one gaining much of an advantage over the other. The two seemed almost perfect foils for one another, though sharing, perhaps, an unspoken mutual respect—something I suspect neither man would be quick to admit.

Correspondence had also flown between Klass and William Moore, a West Coast researcher who, from the start, was deeply involved in the MJ-12 matter. Jaime Shandera, the filmmaker who received the unprocessed roll of film, has remained in the background.

In the contest over authenticity of the MJ-12 document, Phil Klass finally seemed to gain the upper hand. In a "White Paper"[4] dated October 12, 1989,[5] he asserted that a Smith Corona typewriter introduced "around 1963" was used to type the MJ-12 Truman memo of September 24, 1947. The memo, in short, was counterfeit and Klass said he had the word of a professional document examiner to support his claim.

This was not, however, the first MJ-12 paper to be declared counterfeit. A document called the "Aquarius" paper—the first to surface referring to MJ-12—was reported to be a retyped version of an Air Force Office of Special Investigations (AFOSI) teletype message. William Moore made this disclosure during a controversial two-hour talk at the July 1989 Mutual UFO Network (MUFON) symposium in Las Vegas, but we'll come back to this.

Klass believed the signature on the September 24, 1947 Truman memorandum was taken from an authentic memo to Dr. Vannevar Bush, dated October 1, 1947. The authentic signature, he said, was recopied onto the purported September 24 memo, after which it was brushed to eliminate copy lines around the signature and then photocopied a final time. The signatures are identical, said Klass, except for a slight difference in size caused by the photocopying process.

During a telephone conversation, Klass recounted his effort to obtain expert analysis of the September 24 memo, and also related how that task led him to a man who had earlier been consulting with Moore, Friedman, and Shandera.

*　*　*

Klass's initial effort took him to Joe Nickell, of Lexington, Kentucky, whose hobby is the authenticity of documents. Nickell, however, was a member of the executive council of the Committee for the Scientific Investigation of Claims of the Paranormal (CSICOPS), an organization that has been at odds with nearly all segments of the UFO community. Realizing that the pro-UFO faction would hold any opinion by Nickell in great suspicion, Klass asked for a referral. Nickell suggested the Yellow Pages.

Checking the Washington directory, Klass came across the name of David Crown, a handwriting expert and former director of the CIA's document authentication division. "I called Crown [now retired] and he told me the MJ-12 papers had been exposed as a hoax," Klass said.

Crown, a self-described "high-priced talent," referred Klass to a New York document analyst with a known interest in the MJ-12 papers—an analyst identified only as "PT." Klass did not know at the time that PT had earlier consulted with Moore, Friedman, and Shandera. He also did not know that PT had already informed Moore that the Truman memo was probably bogus—information Moore was not yet ready to disclose.[6]

Klass telephoned PT and learned the analyst had a strong interest in seeing a copy of the authentic October 1, 1947 Truman letter. This he mailed via overnight express. There was no mention, at the time, of PT's involvement with Moore, Friedman, and Shandera.

PT made a transparency of the Truman letter for easy enlargement and carried that, Klass said, along with a transparency of the MJ-12 memo (already in PT's possession), to a document examiner's conference in San Francisco.

"A week later [October 12, 1989], PT called me," Klass recalled. The essence of that conversation was that the MJ-12 document, or at least the Truman memo, was certainly counterfeit. PT's conclusion—undisputed by other analysts at the West Coast conference—was based, in part, on a comparison of enlarged copies of the two signatures. But there is more.

Klass also learned that PT had been in touch with a Los Angeles document examiner—another man consulting with Moore, Friedman, and Shandera. Months earlier, this analyst had been permitted to reproduce from the original MJ-12 35mm film. The availability of first-generation copies, enlarged for comparison and study, enabled PT to firmly conclude that the MJ-12 Truman memo was typed with a Smith Corona cartridge machine introduced no earlier than 1963. Clues to determining the typewriter year and model were the capital letters "A" and "W," both of which, Klass said, tended to tear the old-style carbon ribbon. This defect was corrected by Smith Corona in the model introduced in 1963.

* * *

This brings us to William Moore's controversial 1989 Las Vegas talk.[7] Moore revealed that nine years earlier, in September 1980, he had been approached by a man claiming to be a member of the intelligence community. This individual alleged that he and several others in intelligence were unhappy with the United States government's UFO cover-up policy. Moore said he was asked to cooperate with this group, and an arrangement was established through a liaison. Moore identified the liaison as Richard Doty, a former special agent with the Air Force Office of Special Investigations (AFOSI). Doty retired from the Air Force in 1988.

Moore said it soon became apparent he was being "recruited" by the group to supply information on the activities of a number of UFO researchers, but most especially on a researcher named Paul Bennewitz.

A professional physicist, Bennewitz had been privately investigating UFOs and unexplained animal deaths, and in the course of this, and using sophisticated electronic equipment, he reportedly intercepted unusual low-frequency radio signals coming from the Kirtland AFB/Sandia National Labs complex in New Mexico. According to Moore, Bennewitz became convinced that the signals originated with UFOs and not with the government, and he voiced this belief "to virtually anyone." Moore claimed that several government agencies became part of an elaborate campaign to "defuse" and discredit Bennewitz by feeding him bizarre misinformation. As a result of this campaign, Bennewitz came to believe that malevolent aliens were hatching a plan to control the Earth. Moore said he decided to play along in order to try to discover more about the government's knowledge of UFOs.

During the course of this, Moore said he was given a document that he was expected to pass along to Bennewitz. This was the

"Aquarius" paper referred to earlier—a three-page extract of a report supposedly prepared by the mysterious MJ-12 committee. Speaking before MUFON, Moore said the Aquarius paper was a "retyped version" of a "real AFOSI message."[8] He said the document was handed to him in February 1981 with the intention that he pass it to Bennewitz. It was assumed that Bennewitz would take the document to the media as proof of alien invaders—at which point the paper would be exposed as bogus, and Bennewitz would be further discredited.

Moore's disclosure about all of this quite naturally caused pandemonium within the UFO community. More to the point is the fact that his admission about the Aquarius paper, when coupled with information supplied by the document analyst PT and by Philip Klass, seems to indicate that very little about the MJ-12 subject is credible.

★　★　★

Consider: The MJ-12 document surfaced at a time when the Roswell legend had blossomed into a hot topic. Moore and Friedman had already compiled extensive evidence of a forty-year-old occurrence near the community. It is apparent the Army Air Corps was involved—that news reports were issued, and then altered. There is every indication of a major cover-up, but of what? An alien spacecraft? Or was it something else?

Consider: Kenneth Arnold never reported seeing "flying saucers" over the Cascade Mountains two weeks prior to the alleged Roswell crash. His description, at least for the lead object in the formation, was more like that of a flying wing or flying crescent.

Consider also: In 1947 Northrop Corporation had been testing prototype flying-wings for at least a year. Northrop has never released any of the early flying wings for permanent public display. (The two prototypes crashed but a number of other flying wings were built.) It is likely the test models were kept secure because Northrop continued to work with the basic design—leading, ultimately, to the development of the modern B-2 stealth bomber.

Despite all this, I am not saying (nor do I really believe) that an early flying wing crashed in New Mexico in 1947.[9] I use the wing as an example of how little we really know about military research and development during this era. What I am suggesting is that the government had something advanced and experimental in the works—something that may have failed miserably on a stormy night in early July 1947.

In March 1995, the Department of Defense declassified "Silver Bug," a project that had been under wraps since its inception shortly after the Second World War. A report on the project, dated February 15, 1955 and prepared by the Air Technical Intelligence Center at Wright-Patterson AFB, Ohio, reveals plans and designs for a jet-powered, saucer-shaped vehicle, which in theory would ascend vertically and fly at speeds of 2,300 MPH at an altitude of more than eighty thousand feet. The plans were reportedly inspired by designs taken from the Germans at the end of the war. The Germans were unable to complete work on Silver Bug, but it's possible that a fully operational prototype was built and tested in the United States. It is also conceivable that a test flight of the prototype ended in a crash near Roswell.[10]

In the wake of the crash, and with the Kenneth Arnold sighting and subsequent flying saucer reports on everyone's mind, a two-part disinformation scheme was set into motion.

The scheme began with an announcement to radio and press that a flying disc had been recovered. To the media, this implied either a spacecraft or a new type of Russian aircraft (inasmuch as tension between the Soviets and the United States had been building since the end of the war). The second phase was the "cover-up." This involved quashing the "genuine" disc report and replacing it with a clumsy account about a fallen weather balloon. The result was that a segment of the public—accustomed to wartime secrecy—decided the first story was true: a disc—a spaceship, perhaps, or a foreign aircraft—had been recovered. Those who didn't believe in aliens or were unconcerned about the Russians simply accepted the balloon story. Few, then or now, ever considered that the crash might have involved the test of a top-secret U.S. aircraft.

This still leaves us with the witnesses and their descendants, and the stories they've related of abundant alien wreckage, of hieroglyphic-like writing on pieces of wreckage, and of alien bodies recovered at the scene. If these tales are accurate, then the military did a superb job of removing every bit of evidence. Or perhaps the stories are simply not true. Perhaps the witness recollection is a "screen"—a set of false memories implanted by means of drugs and hypnosis, or by an early form of radio-implant technology![11] Then again, perhaps the entire Roswell scenario is simply what some ultimately chose to remember! Arguments can be made for or against every aspect of the Roswell issue, but it all boils down to this: tales of the event are not enough; hard evidence is necessary.

In early 1993, Steven Schiff, a Republican congressman from New Mexico, was asked by several constituents to look into the Roswell story.[12] Schiff took them seriously enough to begin an inquiry. In March 1993 he wrote to then-Secretary of Defense Les Aspin, asking for a personal briefing and a report on all actions regarding Roswell. Schiff received replies from Colonel Larry G. Shockley, of the office of the Assistant Secretary of Defense for legislative affairs, and from Rudy de Leon, Special Assistant to the Defense Secretary. Both men referred Schiff to the National Archives and Record Administration.

Schiff again wrote to Aspin in May and August, and demanded that the Defense Department conduct the necessary research to produce a detailed report. At one point he received a letter from R. Michael McReynolds, director of the textual reference division of the National Archives. McReynolds said the Air Force had turned over to the archives all records of its investigation into UFOs, but nothing in that investigation (Project Blue Book) said anything about Roswell. Schiff's media response was that his search was "not a UFO hunt. This is a file hunt. The idea of alien spacecraft is not my first explanation for any of this. It's possible it was a weather balloon, attended by a public relations fiasco."

In early 1994, Schiff—still unable to get answers—asked Congress' investigative arm, the General Accounting Office, to look into the matter. Meanwhile, the Air Force issued a whole new report of its own on Roswell—reiterating that the crashed object was nothing more than a research balloon.[13] In midsummer 1995, the GAO report was released, but it resolved nothing—the balloon explanation went unaltered. One curious fact of the probe, however, was the discovery that many of the old Roswell Army Air Field records were somehow destroyed. In fact, more than three years worth of records are said to be lost, including any and all RAAF documents from the June to July 1947 period.

In late 1995, the appearance of a bizarre video eclipsed the long-awaited GAO report. Created from 16mm film obtained by a London, England, music promoter named Ray Santilli, the televised video purports to show the autopsy of an extraterrestrial body taken from the Roswell crash site. Santilli said he purchased the film from an unidentified man who claimed he was a military cameraman at Roswell. The film is said to be old stock—possibly 1947 stock. Nonetheless, it is regarded with great suspicion: ufologists, medical experts, and professional filmmakers have all demonstrated serious differences of opinion on whether the film is authentic or an elaborate, expensive hoax.

If authentic, why is it not in government hands? The mysterious cameraman supposedly held back certain canisters of film because of difficulty in processing. Other canisters—the majority, according to the story—were processed and sent directly to Washington. Later, when the problem film was ready, the cameraman reportedly tried—without success—to have his Washington contacts come and get it. Why would they completely disregard the additional film? Why let it pass into the hands of someone who could make it public? Even if long overlooked, the film would certainly have disappeared for good at the first hint of disclosure. If there is a cover-up in place since 1947, then the autopsy film was a tremendous blunder—a major break in an otherwise tightly woven web of security.

* * *

How, exactly, does all this fit with the MJ-12 document? Actually, it's pretty simple.

Whoever masterminded the document (and perhaps even the autopsy film) was simply taking advantage of the Roswell legend and didn't much care whether a UFO crashed near there in 1947 or not. Why? Because no matter what happened at Roswell, it panders to those who wish to believe—it reinforces the already widespread notion that our planet is being visited by extraterrestrials!

Which raises the question: who stands to gain? How about members of the counterintelligence community?

Fostering this sort of belief makes an excellent cover for covert types; they can perform all sorts of unscrupulous activity—abductions and experimentation, for example—and with hypnosis and drugs and radio-implant technology pass it off as the actions of meddling, superior, unstoppable alien beings.

Because a document such as MJ-12 is so nearly believable, even after close scrutiny and when it is found to be wanting, it generates suspicion and frustration among all concerned. In the end no one knows with any certainty what to believe and everyone ends up growling at one another. Indeed, emotional storms such as this have long kept the UFO community in the U.S. so fragmented that its members can seldom hope to achieve anything of significance.

As for the Roswell legend, the only thing for certain is that something happened in the desert in 1947: something important, something requiring military intervention and a heavy mantle of secrecy. The truth, as they say, may be out there, but in this instance it may be well out of reach.

Notes

1. Curt Sutherly, "MJ-12: Evidence of Deception," *Caveat Emptor*, spring 1990, edited by Gene Steinberg, pp. 13–20.

2. *San Francisco Chronicle*, July 9, 1947.

3. Curt Sutherly, "An Interview with Stanton Friedman," *Official UFO*, May 1977.

4. Many of the "White Papers" disseminated by Phil Klass are photocopied letters addressed to those he has challenged. Moore, Friedman, and Doty have all been recipients of such letters.

5. A letter to William Moore.

6. Information about the apparently bogus Truman memo was not released by M., F., & S., according to Moore, because the trio had pursued "several opinions" to lend credibility to their findings. However, these opinions were "mixed." (Letter from Moore to Klass dated October 16, 1989.)

7. William L. Moore's presentation was given July 1, 1989, at the Aladdin Hotel, Las Vegas.

8. Moore allegedly admitted to researcher Richard Hall that he personally did a "cut and paste job" on the Aquarius paper. (Robert Hastings, "The MJ-12 Affair: Facts, Questions, Comments," *MUFON UFO Journal*, June 1989, p. 8.

9. Prototype and experimental aircraft were tested at Muroc Field (Edwards AFB) in 1947, and at China Lake, California. There was no known testing of aircraft in New Mexico.

10. "Roswell Plus 50," an article in the July 1997 *Popular Mechanics* by Jim Wilson, science and technology editor, provides a detailed rundown on Project Silver Bug. Wilson's conclusion about the occurrence near Roswell is unrelated to Silver Bug, however. Instead, he suggests that the crashed object was either a U.S. re-engineered, high-altitude Fugo balloon similar to the incendiary balloons launched by the Japanese during World War II, except that this one was piloted; or that it was a combination high-altitude balloon and aerodynamic lifting body inspired by both German and Japanese wartime technology. He supports these views with clues drawn from various interviews and from declassified documents that refer to still other government projects long kept secret.

11. In September 1989, a lengthy article titled "The Controllers" was submitted to a magazine for editorial consideration. The author, who has since dropped out of sight, reported that since 1947 the U.S. intelligence community has been involved in a series of sophisticated, covert mind-control experiments, and that said experiments might be linked directly to reports of human abductions by aliens. The magazine never published "The Controllers," and the editor's copy was mailed to me. "The Controllers" is compelling and heavily referenced. It is also quite frightening to read, which is one of the reasons it was not published.

   According to the author, attempts at domestic mind control may have started as early as 1947 with Project Chatter, a U.S. Navy program involving drug experimentation. The writer cites no less than six other programs under such names as Artichoke, Bluebird, Pandora, Mkdelta, Mksearch, and Mkultra.

   Experiments conducted under these programs involved memory erasure, truth serums, posthypnotic suggestion, rapid induction of hypnosis, electronic stimulation of the brain (ESB— a form of electronically induced emotional and behavioral control), and microwave induction of intracerebral "voices." In preparing the paper, the author drew from various unclassified books and references, some of them written by former government mind control experimenters. One of the most astonishing revelations in "The Controllers" is that human radio-implant technology existed in crude form as early as the 1950s, and has since been so miniaturized and modernized that, if discovered, the technology might well be accepted as extraterrestrial in origin. The author relates that modern ESB can "be elicited with microwaves and other forms of electromagnetic radiation [and] used with and without electrodes." He also refers to a long rumored technology called RHIC-EDOM ("Radio Hypnotic Intracerebral Control"— "Electronic Dissolution of Memory"). The combination of these techniques, he says, can "remotely induce hypnotic trance, deliver suggestions to the subject, and erase all memory for both the instruction period and the act which the subject is asked to perform." About EDOM specifically, he notes that this is "nothing less than 'missing time' itself"—a phenomenon long recognized in abduction cases.

12. Republican Congressman Steven H. Schiff, 51, died from cancer-related causes on March 26, 1998. Schiff was a colonel in the Air Force Reserve and served on active duty in Bosnia and the Persian Gulf after the war with Iraq.

13. On June 24, 1997, the fiftieth anniversary of Kenneth Arnold's sighting, the Air Force released a second report on the incident near Roswell. The 230-page document, titled "The Roswell Report: Case Closed," provides considerable background on Air Force activities in the vicinity of Roswell from the mid-1940s through the early 1960s. One of the key points of the report was an attempt to explain stories about alien bodies as being nothing more than anthropomorphic dummies dropped by parachute from high-altitude research balloons. However, the dummy tests—meant to determine the best way for astronauts or high-altitude pilots to return safely to earth—were actually conducted years after the incident near Roswell.

CHAPTER 8

Dreamland

BEFORE SUNRISE ON March 6, 1990, the sound of thunder fell over Los Angeles. At an altitude of sixty thousand feet, a black aircraft hurled inland and ripped through a radar "gate," still accelerating.

The aircraft, which had departed a desert air base at 4:30 A.M., had just come from a rendezvous over the ocean with two KC-135 tanker aircraft. After taking on additional fuel, the pilot banked east and lit the engine afterburners. An odd green fire splashed from the exhaust and the black plane—registry number 64-17972—dashed off on its final flight—a hell-raising tear across the continent.

On the East Coast, it was 9:00 A.M. when 17972 hit the gate over Los Angeles. Forty minutes later—titanium skin expanded from the heat of passage and glowing cherry red in front of the cockpit—17972 tore through a gate more than fifteen miles above Kansas City. At the controls was Lt. Col. Raymond E. Yeilding, forty-one, a veteran Air Force pilot. In the reconnaissance systems seat was forty-seven-year-old Lt. Col. Joseph T. Vida.

Six minutes after Kansas City, with ribbon-like silver contrails streaming from the wings and the powerful Pratt & Whitney turbojets operating within normal parameters, 17972 dashed through a gate over St. Louis. Twenty-two minutes later, at 10:08 A.M., the SR-71 "Blackbird" hurled through a final gate near Salisbury, Maryland.[1] On the ground below, a thunderclap greeted those waiting at Washington Dulles International Airport.

At 10:50 A.M. Eastern Standard Time, after a final air refueling, 17972 touched down at Dulles. The Blackbird had just set a new Los Angeles to Washington record as well as a new transcontinental air speed record. The aircraft was now destined for retirement, which in this case was permanent public display at Dulles as part of the Smithsonian's Air and Space Museum; and no one—not the invited members of the media, not the support personnel, or the Air Force brass attending the ceremony—seemed particularly happy about it.

When the final numbers were crunched, they demonstrated that aircraft 64-17972 had shattered the existing cross-country record by more than two and a half hours—an incredible accomplishment, especially for a machine designed in the 1950s and engineered on a slide rule![2] The black plane had clocked through seven radar gates at an average speed of 2,112.52 miles per hour—crossing 2,404 miles in little more than sixty-eight minutes!

* * *

Developed under a top-secret program known as "Senior Crown," the Blackbird—known also as "Habu" (a species of tree viper indigenous to Okinawa)—was operational as early as 1962. In 1964 the aircraft went into production for the Air Force, and its existence—though not its full capability—was revealed on national television by President Lyndon B. Johnson.

Early testing of the SR-71 occurred at a secret air base one hundred miles northwest of Las Vegas, within the sprawling Nellis Range complex. The base has no name or numerous names

Computer image of an **SR-71 "Blackbird."** The Blackbird
was developed under a top-secret program known as "Senior
Crown" and was operational as early as 1962. Testing of the
SR-71 occurred at a secret Nevada air base known today as
Area 51. (U.S. Air Force illustration)

depending on the source of information, and until recently did
not even officially exist. To the public it is best known as Area 51
or "Dreamland." In earlier times it was called "The Ranch" or
"Watertown Strip" (the latter a reference to Groom Dry Lake
Bed along which it is built) and was run by the CIA. In the mid-
1950s the base served as an operational site for the venerable U-2
spy plane. In April 1962, an early version of the SR-71 flew out of
the Groom facility. Known as the A-12, the early Blackbird was a
single-seat aircraft manned by CIA-contracted civilian pilots.

For nearly thirty years a fleet of SR-71s operated globally, mon-
itoring foreign military activity before undergoing official retirement in 1990. Ostensibly, the Blackbird fleet was mothballed for
budgetary reasons and because spy satellites provide a similar
(some would say superior) "look-down" service. In 1994 Congress
forced the Air Force to refurbish and reactivate two Blackbirds.
The planes were declared mission-ready on January 1, 1997. They

were manned by crews from the 9th Reconnaissance Wing at Beale AFB near Sacramento, California, but were actually flown out of the Mojave Desert at Edwards AFB. The reactivated Blackbirds flew for less than a year before the program was again terminated, this time by presidential line-item veto on October 14, 1997.

At the close of the 1990s, only two SR-71s remained in service, both on loan to NASA at Dryden Flight Research Center, Rogers Dry Lake Bed, California, where they were being used as high-altitude test beds in the development of technology for the X-33, the next-generation reusable space vehicle. In contrast, as many as thirty-two Blackbirds were operational during the era of the so-called Cold War.[3] Twelve were lost due to accidents, but according to Paul Crickmore, a British author of two books on the SR-71, not one was ever lost to enemy action.

The effectiveness of the SR-71 was demonstrated early in its career when it flew with impunity over enemy sites in North Vietnam. The North Vietnamese were equipped with Russian built surface-to-air missiles, but the SAMs did not have the speed or range to reach the Blackbird. Habu crew members reported that missiles launched by the North Vietnamese simply fell back to earth.

The SR-71 was so highly classified during the war that even among Air Force rank-and-file it was a legend: everyone talked about it but few people ever saw it. I served with the Air Force during the Vietnam era and saw an SR-71 only once. This occurred during an aircraft flyover honoring a retiring general officer.

The flyover had just concluded and a parade formation on the flight line was dismissed. Those of us on scheduled duty went back to work. I was walking to my assigned aircraft when someone shouted. Turning, I saw an airman in a green fatigue uniform gesturing excitedly toward the control tower. Beyond the tower, coming in low and fast, was a black aircraft.

As a maintenance crew chief, I routinely saw all sorts of aircraft—everything from fighters and bombers to trainer aircraft to cargo transports. I was even present (by sheer chance) when a pair of British Harriers—the fabled vertical takeoff fighters—completed their first nonstop crossing of the Atlantic and touched down softly on a grass median just off an Air Force runway. However, none of this compared with seeing an SR-71.

As the Blackbird passed overhead, mechanics and flight-line personnel craned their necks to stare. The aircraft was unmistakable, even to those who knew of it only from hearsay, and yet it seemed as though something otherworldly was passing overhead. Metal-black and sleek beyond anything else in the sky, the aircraft looked like a spaceship straight out of pulp science fiction.

★　★　★

When the Air Force announced the retirement of the SR-71 in 1990, many observers concluded that the stated reasons—budget constraints and satellite technology—were a ruse. Instead, it was presumed that a new ultrahigh speed reconnaissance aircraft had been developed to replace the aging Blackbird.[4] For a handful of vocal UFO enthusiasts, the Blackbird's departure seemed to validate a long-standing rumor, the rumor being that a new technology had been wrought from the ruin of a crashed extraterrestrial spacecraft. Such stories aside, there were reasons to believe that a new plane was operating in place of the Blackbird. Aviation writers pointed to mysterious donut-on-a-rope jet contrails and unique-signature sonic booms as proof that a revolutionary propulsion system was being tested. They further concluded that the new plane was being flown out of Dreamland—the secret Nevada facility at Groom Dry Lake.

★　★　★

In June 1997, the magazine *Popular Mechanics* reported—in a curious and startling cover story—that the Air Force had abandoned top secret testing at Groom Dry Lake.[5] The story was written by science/technology editor Jim Wilson, who suggested that the operation had been moved to a facility in eastern Utah known as the White Sands Missile Range Utah Launch Complex. Wilson concluded that a military version of NASA's X-33—the next generation space shuttle—would be tested at the Utah facility. He called the site Area 6413, referring to the designation number for the restricted airspace at that location.

To test his theory that the Air Force had pulled out of Groom Lake, Wilson said he drove his rental car into the desert outside Area 51. He saw no civilian security guards—the so-called "cammo dudes" who patrol the perimeter in white Cherokee Jeeps—and instead found a partially washed-out road leading to a security fence and a padlocked cattle gate. On the fence flanking the gate were weather-beaten signs that warned against trespassing. He said he spent fifteen minutes flashing the headlights of his car and sounding the horn, but no one came to investigate.

Wilson's story led me to contemplate just what part of the desert he had traveled into. He had clearly not approached Groom Lake by the main road as there is no gate along that access—only signs warning that "deadly force" may be used to stop trespassers. The signs encountered by Wilson apparently said nothing about deadly force, but they did caution that bombing practice was conducted beyond the padlocked gate. Wilson seemed to take all this to mean that he had approached the base by some kind of "back door," though to me it seemed obvious that he had not approached the base at all—but had arrived, instead, at one of the access points to the vast Nellis bombing and gunnery range that surrounds Area 51 on three sides.[6]

I felt certain of this because six weeks earlier I had been standing just outside the perimeter of Area 51. And although I could not dispute Wilson's reasoning about the Utah site and its possible connection to the X-33 program, I did not share his view that Groom Dry Lake had been abandoned. In fact, at the time of my visit, in April 1997, there was every indication that the base was operational.

* * *

My trip to the outskirts of Area 51 was unexpected. Anthony Benson, at the time a publicist with Llewellyn Publications, had somehow convinced a Los Angeles television producer that I'd be a good interview subject for a series of news reports on unexplained phenomena. Benson arranged airfare to Las Vegas, and also arranged a rental car to take us to the town of Rachel, Nevada, not far from Area 51. The plan was to meet the television producer and her cameraman in Rachel.

As fate would have it, just about the time I received my airline ticket I was taken ill with a flu virus. I spent most of the next five days in bed, more miserable than at any time during the previous ten years. On the day of departure I boarded a "redeye" from Harrisburg to Las Vegas, still sick but grimly determined to make the journey. The flight was a horrible experience and I marvel at my own tenacity (or stupidity) in boarding the plane. The following morning I broke a fever in my hotel room, and later in the day Anthony arrived. Needless to say, we didn't spend a great deal of time checking out the town, although Anthony did give me a tour of Vegas by car and a quick lesson in blackjack. The next morning we loaded the rental with bottles of water, vitamin C, and herbal medicines, and drove northwest into the high desert.

Located in Sand Spring Valley along state Highway 375, the town of Rachel is essentially a collection of mobile homes dating to the early 1970s, when the Union Carbide Company opened a mine on a nearby mountain. Although the mine is now closed, Rachel survives, helped along by tourists drawn to the presence of nearby Groom Lake and by reports of recurring UFO activity in the surrounding desert. In response to all of this, the Nevada State Assembly has designated Highway 375 the "Extraterrestrial Highway." Visitors to Rachel find a combination store and gas station, and a motel that also includes a restaurant and bar. These two establishments provide the only source of public amenities, food, or shelter for miles around.

Owned by Pat and Joe Travis, the motel has had various names through the years, but is known today as the "Little A'Le'Inn." It was here, just outside the motel restaurant, that Anthony and I were greeted by Lonnie Lardner, a reporter and producer for KTLA-TV in Los Angeles, and by Robert Varela, a freelance TV news camera-man. Inside the restaurant, Lonnie and Anthony began discussing plans for the interview while I introduced myself to Chuck Clark, a Rachel resident who has spent years trying to assess the region's UFO activity. An amateur astronomer and a quiet, thoughtful man, Chuck seemed open minded about the UFO phenomenon and not especially anxious to promote one particular theory or explanation. I was impressed with his level-headedness, but before we could talk further it was time to depart for the interview.

With Lonnie and Robert in one vehicle and Anthony and I fol-lowing in the rental, we drove east along Highway 375—retracing our path some twenty miles before arriving at an intersection marked by a large white mailbox. Turning onto a dirt road, we drove south five miles before intersecting another dirt road that traveled west-southwest. This was Groom Lake Road and to our left, in the distance, we could see the rugged Groom range that hides Area 51 to the south. Here we found cattle grazing on sparse vegetation. The TV news team pulled over and Anthony parked the rental behind their vehicle.

Because of the presence of the cattle, Lonnie had decided that this was a good location for an interview about unexplained ani-mal deaths and their possible connection to UFO activity. She and I were soon strolling up and down the shoulder of the road, acting as though it was the sort of thing one does everyday. At one point during the interview I broke into fits of coughing: the dry desert air, as well as the herbal expectorant I had been taking, was clear-ing my respiratory tract. Anthony came to my rescue with a large bottle of water. The interview resumed, though because of my illness I suspect my answers were mostly inadequate or inane. As if to confirm this, one of the steers lowed loudly during a crucial question, giving us all a good laugh afterward.

Back in our vehicles, we drove another ten or twelve miles along Groom Lake Road until we arrived at the buffer zone that surrounds Area 51. Here, large metal signs warned us to go no further or face the possibility of being shot. A half-minute later we had company: "cammo dudes" in a white Jeep Cherokee. The guards, a pair of burly men, had been alerted to our arrival by motion sensors planted along the access road. They parked their Jeep atop a convenient ridge and set up surveillance.

For more than two hours we remained in front of the warning signs while Lonnie asked questions and Robert rolled videotape. Periodically I would back away and break into a fit of coughing, and we would rest while I sipped water to lubricate my throat. Nearby, seated in the shadow of one of the cars or sometimes restlessly pacing, Anthony kept an eye on the security guards who stood watching us from the ridge. I did not envy the guards their vigil. It was hot, and they stood in the open sun wearing desert-toned battle dress uniforms, studying us with a powerful binocular mounted atop a tripod. I felt certain they listened as well—using directional audio gear—and I mentioned this to the others.

The presence of the guards forced me to privately acknowledge that our presence and activity at that place would be documented by the Defense Department. For each of the others, a memorandum would go into a new file or files—unless there had been some prior reason for Uncle Sam to keep an eye on them, in which case the memo would go into an existing file. In my own case, the memorandum would go into an old dossier—a file dating back to my Air Force tour and carried forward to include my current federal service, along with, I suspect, a record of my writings about UFO and fortean phenomena. I had once considered requesting a copy of my file via the Freedom of Information Act, but eventually decided it wasn't worth the effort: I already had a good idea of the content of the record, and if anyone keeping track had any opinion about my activities, so be it.

As the interview progressed and the afternoon lengthened, my arms, neck, and face (foolishly, I wore no hat) began to tingle from the effects of sunburn and windburn. The heat, combined with a throat injured from repeated coughing, made it increasingly difficult to formulate solid responses to Lonnie's questions. By the time the interview concluded, it was after 3:00 P.M. From the rental, Anthony produced snack food and the four of us ate a late lunch of sorts. When we finally prepared to leave, Lonnie waved to the guards, who still kept watch. Surprisingly, they waved back. "Maybe," she said, "we should have invited them down for something to eat."

★　★　★

Backtracking along Groom Lake Road, we reached the juncture with its grazing cattle and turned north onto the road leading to the mailbox and Highway 375. A moment later Robert pulled his car to the shoulder and climbed out, lugging his heavy video camera. He was joined by Lonnie. Anthony parked the rental and we followed. Tossing the camera to his shoulder and adjusting the lens, Robert began shooting video of the Groom Range and the fronting desert landscape. I found myself wishing I had brought along one of my 35mm cameras: the Groom Mountains had a wild beauty that would have worked well framed in black and white.

Studying the landscape, I noticed a billowing cloud of dust back the way we had come. I pointed this out to Anthony, and suggested that it might be our friends in the Jeep.

Distances are hard to judge in the desert: objects that appear reasonably near can often be miles away. The vehicle generating the dust cloud had closed to within half a mile before we realized that it was a large white bus of a kind commonly used by the military. As it drew nearer, Robert aimed his video camera. The bus roared past, not turning—staying its course on Groom Lake Road.

It bore no external markings and each window was painted black. As it moved away at a speed of no less than sixty miles per hour, I realized that the bus was carrying employees from the base.

Several hours and one speeding ticket later (given by a Nevada trooper who seemed unusually curious about our recent where-abouts), Anthony and I were back in Las Vegas, and by noon the following day I was waiting to board a return flight to Pennsylvania. Sitting in the airport terminal, I had time to reflect upon the questions Lonnie had asked and on my response to those questions.

One question in particular cut to the heart of the interview: what, precisely, did I think was going on inside Area 51? My reply had been a weary, sarcastic comment about top-secret aerospace research. A good reporter, Lonnie had of course not let it go at that, and her next question pursued the inevitable UFO connection.

★   ★   ★

If we accept legend, then we accept that a long time ago a wrecked alien starship was collected by the military and hauled away to a secret test facility. In early versions of the legend, the alien craft was installed in a heavily guarded hanger at Wright-Patterson AFB in Dayton, Ohio. However, time and retelling have placed the ship in a heavily guarded hanger at Area 51. In either case, the spaceship is said to be undergoing a process called "reverse engineering," which involves taking the vehicle apart and studying it in order to duplicate or partially adopt the technology. Reverse engineering has been successfully applied to captured foreign aircraft, such as with high performance Russian-built MIG fighters; but despite all the rumors and nonsense to be found in books, on television, and on that great gossip network, the Internet, I doubt this same process has been applied to an alien space vehicle, and I said as much to Lonnie.

Think me naive, if you will, but the existence of Area 51 does not imply the presence of captured spaceships or dead (or alive) ET crew members. Granted, the security at Groom Lake is tight and sophisticated, but the place is a top-secret research facility and hugely important to the Defense Department and the multibillion-dollar aerospace industry. Security in such a place is expected to be uncommonly tight. Still, no amount of security or secrecy is ever absolute.

In May 1997, the magazine *Popular Science* published a cover story that appeared to shed light on at least some of the secret activity at Area 51. The article—an interesting mix of source material and historical data—examined government research into aircraft invisibility (visual cloaking and not radar invisibility) and described experiments founded on a deceptively simple premise: adjust the external color and lighting of an aircraft to match the surrounding sky, and you cause the plane to become "invisible" against the sky.[7] This idea was first proven during the Second World War with airplanes illuminated by sealed beam lamps, and again during the Vietnam War using a similar technique.

Steve Douglass and Bill Sweetman, the writers of the *Popular Science* piece, reported that in newer tests electrically charged polymer panels replaced the older sealed beam lamps. When the voltage level was altered, the panels changed color to shades of blue, white or gray, causing the aircraft to blend into the sky. A variation of this process—tested at Groom Lake, according to the writers (who understandably did not cite their source)—produced a "flickering skin" effect that, in theory, could prevent state-of-the-art missiles from homing onto their target.

Aircraft invisibility is undoubtedly only one of many aviation and aerospace research projects underway at Area 51. Others would likely include the testing of unmanned, computer-controlled (autonomous) aerial combat vehicles and ever more sophisticated manned aircraft—including the successor to the SR-71.[8]

* * *

In 1993, the Testor Corporation of Rockford, Illinois—a leading manufacturer of model airplanes—unveiled a new model called the "Aurora"—the long-rumored Blackbird replacement.[9] The designer was aviation writer-historian John Andrews, who earlier in his career had twice surprised the Defense Department with his ability to unearth and duplicate top-secret aircraft design.

In the late 1950s, Andrews created an accurate model of the secret U-2 spy plane. He kept it out of production at the request of the Defense Department, and the model was unveiled only after a U-2 flown by Gary Powers was shot down over the Soviet Union in 1960. In 1986 he did it again with a model version of the secret F-117 stealth fighter. The DOD responded by emphatically denying that any such airplane existed.

In 1993, his "Aurora" model provoked yet another strong denial. A two-stage design, the Aurora concept was unique: a black, triangular craft attached to a larger SR-71-style lifting body. At full scale, Andrews estimated that the larger aircraft would measure about 160 feet in length, and the triangular vehicle about 80 feet.

The larger aircraft, which Testor Corporation called the SR-75, could in theory accelerate to 3.5 times the speed of sound while carrying the smaller vehicle on its back. The smaller aircraft, referred to as the XR-7, would separate from the main craft in the upper atmosphere and accelerate to seven times the speed of sound—more than 5,000 miles per hour—pushed along by a new engine technology referred to as "pulse detonation wave."

Industry analysts believe pulse detonation engines not only exist, but are responsible for the strange donut-on-a-rope contrails that first appeared over southern California in 1991—a year after the SR-71 was retired. The contrails have since been observed in various other locations, including Pennsylvania, where I saw one in 1995.

The sun was setting and the vapor trail was already dissipating as I drove to my apartment. I noticed the trail only because it was directly in front of me, above the horizon and illuminated by the sun's afterglow as I crested a hill. The rings encircling the main trail were clearly evident, and only later did I become aware—through photos and televised reports—that this was not an aberration but an indication of what seemed to be a new aircraft engine technology.

The donut-on-a-rope contrails are not, however, the only indication of a new ultrahigh-speed plane. In 1991 and 1992, U.S. Geological Survey seismic stations on the West Coast recorded aerial shock waves that traveled inland from the Pacific Ocean at three times the speed of sound. Each boom occurred on a Thursday at 7:00 a.m., eliminating the possibility that they were random natural phenomena. A USGS researcher named Jim Mori compared the signature of the booms with those of the SR-71 and the Space Shuttle, and found that they were completely different.

★   ★   ★

The existence of a new high-speed plane was further suggested, beginning about 1990, by an outbreak of reports of triangle-shaped UFOs. In many cases, the objects were similar in description to the Testor XR-7. In the United States, aviation analysts suspected that the Lockheed "Skunk Works" in Palmdale, California, was developing a secret plane. This was the same shop that created both the SR-71 and the F-117 stealth fighter. Lockheed was noncommittal about any such project and referred inquiries to the Air Force. The Air Force said the plane did not exist. In Great Britain, aviation experts suspected that British Aerospace at Warton, Lancashire was working on a triangular aircraft known as HALO (High Altitude, Low Observable). British Aerospace denied this, and the Ministry of Defence said the HALO project did not exist.

As the debate and conjecture continued, so too did the sightings of triangle-shaped UFOs. However, in most cases the reported objects did not behave like conventional aircraft, except in the sense that they appeared in the sky. They behaved like . . . well, like UFOs.

Witnesses in the town of Steelton, Pennsylvania, were faced with this conundrum in July 1994. On the night of Tuesday, July 26, numerous residents observed a dark triangle-shaped object as it flew silently overhead. The object was illuminated by a pattern of lights on the underside and two bright "head lamps" at the front or leading portion of the triangle. A story about the sighting in the next day's *Harrisburg Patriot News* speculated that the UFO was a new kind of stealth aircraft. If so, it was an astoundingly slow stealth aircraft—traveling at about fifteen miles per hour, or about half the speed of the original Wright Flyer.

During the 1980s, similar slow-moving, nocturnal UFOs appeared repeatedly over the New York Hudson River Valley.[10] Many of the objects displayed lighting patterns in the shape of a boomerang or a flying wing. On November 22, 1989, the Air Force publicly unveiled its B-2 stealth bomber—a large flying wing. Skeptics, and those not familiar with the complexity of the UFO phenomenon, concluded that the mysterious objects in New York and elsewhere were secret night tests of the B-2. Unfortunately, the B-2 does not have the capability to fly at extremely slow speeds or fly in total silence. Nor does it hover, as was the case with many Hudson Valley UFOs. The B-2 is "stealthy" only in the sense that it is dark in color and virtually invisible to radar at a distance.

Furthermore, the appearance of slow moving, brightly illuminated UFOs over heavily populated areas is not consistent with the testing of top-secret aircraft. In fact, it suggests quite the opposite: that someone or something wants to be seen! There are other problems as well, such as the oft-reported ability of UFOs to disappear or "blink out" and almost immediately reappear somewhere else, or to speed away at what is clearly a supersonic pace, and do either of these things without triggering a sonic boom (which means they do not displace air). The technology needed to do this would have to be based on something like quantum mechanics and not on classical physics, and at our present level of science this puts us—for all intents and purposes—into the realm of magic.

There is, however, another possibility.

The lobby of the Trade Winds Inn, Fort Smith, Arkansas, during the first **International UFO Conference** in 1975. (Photo by the author)

Let's assume that UFOs are not the product of some nearly magical alien technology, and let's further assume that some of them are not even solid objects. Instead, they might be a kind of advanced holography—a three-dimensional imagery so exact that it would appear to be real, or at least real enough to fool a surprised observer.

Commercial holography is still primitive, little more than a toy and certainly nowhere near the level of technology envisioned in film and television science fiction, most notably *Star Trek*. Nonetheless, the existence of sophisticated holographic projectors or emitters—employed from hidden ground locations or from conventional aircraft—cannot be dismissed inasmuch as military research and development is always well ahead of commercial application. Of course, if advanced holographic apparatus do exist and are being employed to create UFO images, this would imply a deliberate deception—leading us into areas of dark speculation.

★   ★   ★

In 1975, while attending the first International UFO Conference at Fort Smith, Arkansas, I met a gentleman named Jim Oberg. I was seated in a crowded restaurant at the Trade Winds Inn, the site of the conference. The place was literally packed with scientists, engineers, and UFO enthusiasts. Oberg approached and introduced himself, and asked if he could share my table.

Over lunch I learned that, beyond a mutual interest in the UFO phenomenon, Oberg and I were in attendance for essentially the same reason: we were each on story assignment for a newsstand magazine. I liked the man at once as he exhibited a certain humor and brilliance. I also discovered that he was skeptical about one of the more popular UFO viewpoints, notably the belief that UFOs are of extraterrestrial origin.

Many years have passed since my one and only encounter with Jim Oberg, and I have followed his career with interest. He continues to write on science issues and has become widely recognized as an expert on both the American and Russian space programs. During space missions, Oberg has been quoted by the press and consulted by the media.

In 1997, Oberg drafted an open letter to Dr. Steven Greer, head of the Center for the Study of Extraterrestrial Intelligence (CSETI). At the time, Greer and CSETI had organized a public demonstration in Washington, D.C., to decry government secrecy on UFOs, and Oberg addressed this matter. His written observations were insightful and important, and significant with regard to matters covered in this and other chapters. I quote portions of his letter as follows, reprinted from Jim Moseley's *Saucer Smear:*

> I applaud CSETI's efforts . . . and fully support the call for a government declaration that all legal constraints against [UFO] disclosure be dissolved . . . But don't stop merely with legalizing disclosure of all—if any—government secrets about "real UFOs." I believe there is a far more valuable body of "secrets" that will help [us]

understand the decades of UFO phenomena that the
world has experienced. This deals with government-
related activities which directly or indirectly led to public perceptions that UFOs might be real when they
weren't. Sometimes these actions were carefully orchestrated in advance; sometimes they were . . . impromptu
ad hoc damage-limiting tactics. But from my own experience, they seem to have played a tremendous and
widely unappreciated role in inciting and enflaming
public interest in UFOs while deflecting public attention from real highly classified government activities.

I'm referring to situations where government representatives—officials, military officers, etc.—used "UFO"
as a convenient camouflage for other official classified
activities (such as retrieval of crashed aircraft or nuclear
weapons or other objects), or used artificial "UFO" stories (in oral, written, photographic form, etc.) as "trac-
ers" in studying the function of security safeguards and
personnel psychological responses; or used "UFO" as an
excuse (either intended or accidental) to cover up
improper, forbidden, or diplomatically delicate activities
(such as aviation incidents involving dangerous, accidental or deliberate, close passes or intercepts of civilian air-
liners; or overseas excursions of agents on intelligence
missions where deflection of local perceptions are useful; or to conceal from the country of origin the possession of foreign military hardware); or played pranks and
jokes on intended or accidental targets; or any other
activity that the government—or any part of it—wanted
to keep hidden, knowing that having it thought of as
"UFO related" would consign it to the never-never land
of myth and nuttiness, thus keeping mainstream media
attention to a minimum. And it has worked![11]

Oberg completed his letter by noting that any formal demand
for the release of secret UFO information should also include a
demand that immunity be granted to any or all government personnel willing to speak publicly about UFO disinformation prac-
tices. With immunity secured, Oberg said he would be able to

release his own list of individuals who have spoken with him privately, and "who were involved in government activities leading to a number of well-known 'UFO' cases." The list, he said, would "help the public understand where and how much of today's UFO mythology originated."

Unfortunately, and despite Oberg's well-thought-out proposal, it may be too late for any government-related UFO disclosure, no matter how thorough or convincing. Too many people already believe that UFOs are spacecraft piloted by extraterrestrials, and that a few such ships—being either wrecked or disabled—are now hidden at Area 51 along with the bodies of their crew. This viewpoint has become so prevalent, in fact, that virtually no amount of data or testimony to the contrary is going to alter it any time soon. Meanwhile, the fact that the UFO phenomenon is still an unsolved mystery is being lost in a mythology that continually grows and changes, and which—in the process—often seems little more than a colossal, cosmic deceit.

Notes

1. Although the official top speed of the SR-71 is said to be about Mach Three (three times the speed of sound), aerospace insiders estimate that the Blackbird is capable of an easy Mach Four. During the speed dash from Los Angeles to Washington, aircraft 17972 never exceeded normal engine operational limits. The record-breaking coast-to-coast run was set at a pace that in all likelihood was somewhat less than the full capability of the aircraft.

2. Kelly Johnson and Johnson's chief engineer, Ben Rich, designed the SR-71 during the 1950s at the famed Lockheed "Skunk Works." During a February 1990 interview published in the *Washington Post*, Rich told reporter Patrick J. Sloyan that his only computing tool in designing and engineering the Blackbird was a slide rule.

3. "Blackbird," *Air Force* magazine, February 1998 (Vol. 81, No. 2), p. 59.

4. Although early versions of the SR-71 Blackbird have been mothballed, it has long been rumored that newer, faster versions of the aircraft continue to fly. Judith and Garfield Reeves-Stevens, the authors of numerous novels including several *Star Trek* collaborations with William Shatner, fictionalize this view in their tech-suspense thriller *Icefire* (Pocket Books, 1998).

5. Jim Wilson, "The New 'Area 51'," *Popular Mechanics*, June 1997, pp. 54–59.

6. On page 41 of his well-written, self-published *Area 51 & S-4 Handbook*, Chuck Clark notes that the Nellis Bombing Range "includes all of the area surrounding Area 51 on the south, east, and north . . ." Additional information about the handbook and its availability can be obtained by contacting Clark at HCR 61, Box 43, Rachel, NV 89001.

7. Steve Douglass and Bill Sweetman, "Hiding in Plane Sight," *Popular Science*, May 1997, pp. 54–59.

8. Robert H. Williams, "Unmanned Combat Aircraft Age is Rapidly Approaching," *National Defense*, January 1998 (Vol. LXXXII, No. 534), pp. 22–23. The article examines the future of unmanned aircraft that are expected to outfly and outmaneuver manned combat aircraft.

9. The name "Aurora" was discovered in a 1984 Pentagon document alongside proposed budgets for the U-2 and SR-71 spy planes. A former "Skunk Works" boss has stated that Aurora was actually a funding item for the top-secret B-2 stealth bomber.

10. J. Allen Hynek, Philip J. Imbrogno, and Bob Pratt, *Night Siege: The Hudson Valley UFO Sightings* (St. Paul, Minnesota: Llewellyn Publications, 1998).

11. *Saucer Smear* (Vol. 44, No. 6), June 20, 1997.

CHAPTER 9

Dark Moons, Red World

SOMEWHERE IN SPACE, presumably near Mars and possibly even in Mars orbit, is a dysfunctional robot spacecraft—a one billion dollar spacecraft, the *Mars Observer*. And somewhere on the planet's surface, perhaps near the south polar ice cap, is an equally dysfunctional robot, the Polar Lander.

Launched from Florida on September 25, 1992, the *Mars Observer* spent nearly a year coasting through space, arriving in the neighborhood of Mars on August 21, 1993. Equipped with numerous backup systems and fail-safes, it was the most sophisticated machine ever sent to the Red Planet, and the first United States probe directed to Mars in seventeen years. It was scheduled to enter orbit on August 24, 1993, and then spend the next seventy-five days maneuvering into a near-polar orbit 234 miles high.

From polar orbit, the *Observer* was programmed to activate its instruments and conduct a photo-reconnaissance of the entire planet. It was also programmed to take extensive readings of the surface and measurements of the thin Martian atmosphere.

Artist rendition of the **robot spacecraft** *Mars Observer,*
which vanished on August 24, 1993 while attempting to
orbit the Red Planet. (NASA illustration)

As the *Observer* approached the Red Planet, its radio was turned
off so that a filament in a delicate transmitter tube would be protected during pressurization of the thruster fuel tanks. When the
time came for the transmitter to be turned back on, there was only
silence. With the deadline slipping by for entering orbit, mission
engineers signaled the *Observer* to activate its backup transmitter.[1]
There was no response. Then, hoping the craft had entered orbit
but was unable to receive commands (due, perhaps, to a faulty radio
receiver), they waited—knowing that after five days and no message
from Earth, the *Observer* was programmed to radio mission control
and ask, in effect, "Why aren't you talking to me?"[2] Again, there
was only silence as another unmanned probe was lost near Mars.

★   ★   ★

In March 1989, the Russian Mars probe, *Fobos 2*, went mysteriously silent. But unlike the *Mars Observer*, *Fobos 2* sent back a

string of data and a number of photographs before mission control in Kaliningrad lost contact. Some of these photos revealed "enigmatic" objects and surface features that continue to puzzle space scientists.

At the time, journalists in the United States joked that perhaps the Red Star was not compatible with the Red Planet.[3] The Russians had already lost *Fobos 1*, the companion craft to *Fobos 2*, and questions were raised about the level of competence of this latest Mars venture.

Indeed, the history of unmanned exploration of Mars has been, for the Russians, one of frequent misfortune. As early as 1963 the Soviet probe, *Mars 1*, went dead at a distance of about 133 million miles from the sun. In 1965, the Soviet probe, *Zond 2*, went dead, this time at a distance of about 128 million miles from the sun. Neither craft was ever heard from again.[4] Other Russian probes to follow either encountered difficulty or vanished.

While the loss of these probes posed a huge setback for the Russians, the problem was not uniquely theirs. Spacecraft launched by the United States were also going awry en route to Mars.

In 1964, the United States *Mariner 3* failed shortly after liftoff. The following year the *Mariner 4* experienced control problems in roughly the same area of space as the *Mars 1* and *Zond 2*. Fortunately, in this case, control was reestablished and *Mariner 4* went on to be a success—but trouble struck again four years later, in July 1969. This time it was with the *Mariner 7*, intended to fly within two thousand miles of the Red Planet. Engineers at the Jet Propulsion Laboratory (JPL) in Pasadena, California, suddenly lost contact with the craft. Then, some seven hours later the probe came alive, though its ability to transmit data was somewhat decreased and its velocity slightly increased![5]

At the time this occurred, two reporters for *Time* magazine, Don Neff and David Lee, were covering the *Mariner 7* mission. In their rather fertile imagination, this latest occurrence suggested the presence of a "great galactic ghoul" sitting in space near Mars.

The ghoul, they decided, had eaten the earlier Soviet probes and swallowed *Mariner* 7, but for some reason didn't like the taste and spit it back out.[6] Today the Great Galactic Ghoul is a joke that has become something of a space-age legend.

Like ancient mariners confronted with vanishing ships and uncharted oceans who wrote on their maps "Beyond This Place There Be Dragons," or like the test pilots of the 1940s who spoke of a sonic "wall in the sky" that prevented aircraft from going faster than sound, the explorers of space (and those who chronicle them) are giving rise to new myths and legends. No one takes the ghoul seriously, but neither can anyone dismiss the fact that something odd has happened out near Mars.

★ ★ ★

On the night of August 11, 1877, astronomer Asaph Hall perched himself at the eyepiece of the newly completed twenty-six-inch telescope at the United States Naval Observatory, Washington, D.C., and pointed it in the direction of Mars. Hall was searching for two Martian moons that had long been described in legend and folklore. That night, unlike previous nights, his efforts paid off as he spotted a faint object not far from Mars itself.

Unfortunately for Hall, the weather became overcast later that evening and it wasn't until the night of August 16, 1877 that he was again able to locate the object, which proved to be a Martian satellite. On the following night, August 17, Hall made an additional discovery—another satellite even closer to the Red Planet. He named the outer moon Deimos, and the inner one Phobos.

In 1944, another United States Naval Observatory astronomer, B. P. Sharpless, began gathering together all the available observational data on the moons of Mars.[7] His intention was to determine, as best as possible, the orbits of the two satellites. What he discovered was a surprise.

Sharpless found that the inner moon, Phobos, appeared to be in a very gradually decaying orbit. In astronomical parlance, this is called "secular acceleration." Artificial satellites undergo secular acceleration—falling slowly at first but gradually picking up speed—until they meet a fiery end in the Earth's atmosphere. Sharpless, who later reexamined his calculations, remained convinced that Phobos was in a slow, decaying orbit. Despite this, the matter was given little serious consideration and eventually dismissed as so much astronomical gossip.

★ ★ ★

In July 1988, the former Soviet Union launched *Fobos 1* and *Fobos 2* from the Baikonur Cosmodrome.[8] The two probes were the most advanced ever sent by that nation, costing roughly $480 million. At first all went well during the two hundred-day mission, but during a scheduled talk with *Fobos 1* on September 2, 1988, the craft failed to respond. Later, the Russians said the problem was caused by a mistaken command relayed by a radio operator. A month passed while they tried to restore communications, to no avail.

The backup craft, *Fobos 2*, meanwhile, continued on toward Mars without difficulty. En route, the robot vehicle studied the composition of the "solar wind"—the charged particles blowing from the Sun, which theorists believe could be used to power manned craft harnessed to huge mirrored sails. Also studied were the characteristics of interplanetary shockwaves and the location of gamma ray outbursts. Arriving at Mars, *Fobos 2* entered a temporary orbit. Had all gone as planned, it would have later shifted to an "observational" orbit in order to begin a study of the moon Phobos—the main mission target.

★ ★ ★

Along with Deimos, its sister moon, Phobos has been of interest to the Russians since about 1960. That year the astrophysicist I. S. Shklovskii began to reexamine discoveries made by the astronomer Sharpless. The Russian was puzzled by the earlier man's findings. He did not dispute them, but in trying to understand the decaying orbit, he eliminated one possible cause after another. He ruled out the influence of the gravitational fields of Mars and the sun on the orbit of the moon. And he calculated that, at ten miles across, Phobos should be too massive to be dragged down by the thin Martian atmosphere. What's more, Mars has no known magnetic field to influence the moon. The only explanation, Shklovskii finally reasoned, was that Phobos has a very low density; it is not as massive as it appears, and is thus susceptible to atmospheric drag.

Slowed by this drag, Shklovskii speculated that Phobos would creep toward Mars—the onset of secular acceleration. But when the scientist calculated the necessary value, he found the impossible. In order to be affected by the thin Martian atmosphere, Phobos would need a density akin to one one-thousandth the density of water.[9] Since there is no natural substance with such a low density, he concluded that Phobos had to be hollow—and therefore, perhaps artificial!

In his book, *The Cosmic Connection*, astronomer Carl Sagan made the following observations:[10]

> With such a low density, there was only one conclusion possible. Phobos had to be hollow. A vast hollow object 10 miles across could not have arisen by natural processes. Shklovskii, therefore, concluded that it was produced by an advanced Martian civilization. Indeed, an artificial satellite 10 miles across requires a technology far in advance of our own.[11]

In 1971, the unmanned *Mariner 9* spacecraft achieved Mars orbit—arriving, unfortunately, at a time when the Red Planet's surface was masked by a massive dust storm. For Sagan, the storm proved a blessing as he was able to convince NASA to swing the camera scan platforms of the spacecraft toward the Martian moons. Prior to this, Sagan had spent a year lobbying space administration officials to allow him to look at the two moons. NASA had been reluctant to change the Mariner mission profile, and Sagan's request would most likely never have been granted had it not been for the unexpected dust storm.[12]

On the night of November 30, 1971, Sagan and a former student, Dr. Joseph Veverka, for the first time were able to observe close-up photographs of Phobos. After the image was computer enhanced, Sagan pronounced the moon as looking "not so much like an artificial satellite as a diseased potato." He described the orbiting moon as battered, extensively cratered, and "probably billions of years old." He added, "There is no sign of technology on it."[13]

Additional photographs of the moon later did reveal something unusual: a system of linear surface grooves, each about one-third mile across and roughly parallel. These grooves, geologists decided in 1978, are probably "surface manifestations of deep-seated fractures," though the actual cause of the fractures is still unknown.[14]

Five years after *Mariner 9* sent back the first revealing photographs, the mass of Phobos was measured for the first time during a series of flybys made by the *Viking I* spacecraft.[15] Based on this measurement, the density was determined to be quite low, though not nearly as low as was calculated by Shklovskii. Not enough, at any rate, to support a theory that Phobos is completely hollow. *Viking I* also observed that Phobos and its sister moon, Deimos, are both extremely dark in color.

The information on color and density, along with other data transmitted by the probe in May 1977, led scientists to conclude that the moons are made of water-rich carbonaceous chondrite. Found only in the most primitive of meteorites, carbonaceous chondrite is possibly the nearest thing to the original dust from which the moons and planets were formed. Meteors made of the stuff are thought to originate in the asteroid belt between Mars and Jupiter. If Phobos and Deimos are made of carbonaceous chondrite, then they probably originated in the belt and were later captured by Mars.

* * *

More than two thousand asteroids, or minor planets, have been identified out in the dark space between Mars and Jupiter. They range in size from a few miles to more than six hundred miles in diameter, and there are certainly many still undiscovered. The asteroids may once have been part of a larger whole, a major planet. The Martian moons, Phobos and Deimos, may be two pieces of the debris from that world.

The belief that a planet once existed between Mars and Jupiter is an old one, though there is another more recent view—a theory that asteroids are pieces of a world that never fully formed. While no one really knows which view (if either) is correct, the destroyed world theory seems to be the more popular of the two notions. Its proponents suggest that a planet orbiting between Mars and Jupiter exploded, or was struck by another large body (possibly a comet), sending fragments hurtling into surrounding space. How long ago this may have happened is anyone's guess—millions, or billions, of years may have passed in the interim. Of the many fragments, some—a few, perhaps—had sufficient kinetic energy to begin a slow drift toward the sun. Along the way they encountered Mars, and two of the asteroids were snared by that gravitational field and drawn into orbit, becoming the moons Phobos and Deimos. There is, however, another possibility.

According to the NASA report "Mars as Viewed by Mariner 9," meteorites and asteroids are frequently light in color. The Martian moons are extremely dark and evidently of a different composition—the carbonaceous chondrite which, in meteorites of that composition, contains up to twenty percent water.[16] Now, suppose for a moment that, ages ago, Mars was inhabited. A higher intelligence on the planet would have noticed the passing asteroids and almost certainly coveted their value. To the resident population, the asteroids would have been a tremendous boon—a source of water and raw material.

A sufficiently advanced people would have been able to shepherd the asteroids into a stable orbit, and then begin extensive percolation and mining operations to extract water and raw ore. The moons would have been riddled with mine tunnels, thus accounting for the low density revealed during the *Mariner 9* flybys and, in part, vindicating Shklovskii. The fact that our space probes have spotted no evidence of this does not eliminate the possibility. If the significant tunneling, engineering, and mining were done deep in the stone, need there be much evidence on the surface?

The idea that someone may have been mining or excavating small worlds in our solar system is not new. For years rumors have persisted about the discovery of this sort of activity on Earth's own satellite.

In the 1970s, a writer named George H. Leonard compiled a book boldly titled *Somebody Else is on the Moon*.[17] Leonard claimed that a thorough study of NASA photographs revealed the presence of alien machinery on the lunar surface. Also revealed, he said, were changes deliberately made in the landscape, and some suspicion of mining or excavating activities. He cited an anonymous informant: an engineer with a Ph.D. in physics formerly employed by NASA. The mystery informant supported Leonard's claim (perhaps a little too conveniently) by explaining that he and others working for NASA were well aware of something odd occurring on the Moon. Leonard concluded that it was the suspicion or discovery of this alien presence that triggered the space race between the United States and the former Soviet Union.

Some years prior to the release of Leonard's book, in 1971, I was told of an unusual occurrence during one of the manned Apollo lunar missions. At the time I was an Air Force sergeant, and the man telling the story a former astronaut who shall go unnamed. The astronaut said that on this particular mission the main craft entered lunar orbit and the Lander vehicle separated and began its descent. During the descent, the Lander maintained normal radio communication with the orbiting command vehicle. Then something unexpected happened.

The astronaut noted that bizarre sounds, like fire engine sirens, singing, and a generally unintelligible chatter broke in on the restricted NASA radio band. Later, when the Lander was en route back to the command module, the strange interference ceased. However, when the Apollo crew radioed Houston and asked if Mission Control had monitored the unusual racket, the response was, in effect: "No, if you're picking up strange sounds, they're local in nature."

Years later, I learned that some of these odd noises were believed by NASA technicians to be interference between the command module's and Lander's VHF radios. But that explanation doesn't take into account the variety and absurdity of the sounds described by the astronaut.

During the mid-1970s, I experienced an identical noise phenomenon. While discussing a story idea with an editor by telephone, the long-distance call was suddenly interrupted by a barrage of sound— a combination of loud chattering mixed with bell tones, sirens, and much more. The noise was frightening and for a moment made conversation impossible. When it ceased, the editor thanked me for my time and abruptly hung up.

★　★　★

Since 1898, when H. G. Wells' *War of the Worlds* caught the imagination of the English literary set, stories about Mars have been a staple of science fiction. The John Carter novels of Edgar Rice Burroughs, Robert Heinlein's *Red Planet*, Ray Bradbury's *The Martian Chronicles*, and Ben Bova's *Mars* are but a few of the novels and short stories written about our mysterious neighbor in space.

A far older work of fiction—Jonathan Swift's legendary satire, *Gulliver's Travels*—contains a startling reference to the moons of Mars. While the reference is quite brief, no more than a half-paragraph, it is astounding in that Swift's book was originally published in 1726—more than 150 years before the discovery of the two moons by astronomer Asaph Hall!

In Part III of his lengthy satire, Swift places his hero, Gulliver, on the floating island of Laputa, where astronomers are hard at work mapping the heavens.[18] Of the astronomers and their work, Gulliver proclaims:

> They have made a catalogue of ten thousand fixed stars
> . . . They have likewise discovered two lesser stars, or
> "satellites," which revolve about Mars, whereof the
> innermost is distant from the center of the primary
> planet exactly three of his diameters, and the outermost
> five; the former revolves in the space of ten hours, and
> the latter in twenty-one and an half . . .

Most modern scholars believe Swift "borrowed" his information about the Martian satellites from calculations made by Johannes Kepler, the sixteenth-century discoverer of the laws of planetary motion, who is also frequently credited with having discovered the moons of Mars. However, Kepler merely speculated that Mars had two moons; he based this on a belief that since Venus had no moons and Earth had one, then Mars, accordingly, should have two. Out of this grew a belief that each consecutive planet in the solar system possessed one additional moon. This belief was reinforced when the four largest moons of Jupiter were discovered. Mercury was still unknown, and the (hypothetically) ruined fifth planet, where the asteroid belt is located, would have had three moons by this method of reasoning. Today we know this planetary "law" is nonsense, but Kepler couldn't have known that.

This, however, creates a paradox: if Kepler didn't have specific information pertaining to the two Martian moons, then how did Swift come by the calculations given in *Gulliver's Travels?* To restate, he has the inner moon traveling about the planet in ten hours, and the outer moon in twenty-one and one-half hours. The actual orbital time for each moon is: Phobos, seven hours, thirty-nine minutes; Deimos, thirty hours, eighteen minutes.

In an article published in *Pursuit*, the journal of the Society for the Investigation of the Unexplained, former editor Robert J. Durant writes: "Swift's accuracy leaves something to be desired, but his figures are nevertheless 'in the ballpark.' One familiar with the history [of that era of astronomy] would be slow to fault Swift."[19]

Possibly there is an ancient record somewhere documenting the orbit and position of each Martian moon. Outside of recent times, our knowledge of history is terribly incomplete; what we know of our own distant past is largely guesswork propped up by a carefully cultivated belief structure. We may have climbed and fallen time and again, with each civilization rediscovering the knowledge of the past. The solar system may have been mapped and explored, and even colonized, in an earlier age. Evidence of this, if any, would probably be found on Mars or on either of its two tiny moons.

*   *   *

Discoveries claiming the existence of ancient, highly advanced civilizations have never met with much enthusiasm from the scientific community. Most are quietly brushed aside and conveniently forgotten. One example is the controversial Piri Re'is map (a detailed, global chart dating to ancient times) discovered during the early part of the twentieth century.[20] This map and innumerable artifacts found through the years provide strong evidence of earlier advanced societies. But did these early civilizations originate on Earth, or somewhere else? The "ancient astronaut" champions would have us believe that humanity originated elsewhere in the galaxy and settled here, or at least visited Earth for a time—planting the seeds of civilization. This is possible but not likely. If *Homo sapiens* did come from space, need the world of origin have been very far away?

Consider: About twelve thousand years ago Mars may have been in the midst of a processional summer; the planet may have been far warmer than it is today, with a heavier atmosphere capable of sustaining life of the order now found on Earth. This is not a vague speculation, but rather an idea that has been entertained by planetary scientists and supported by more recent findings.[21] At some point an ice age began, accompanied by greatly lowered surface pressure. Liquid water started to vaporize, and eventually much of the Martian atmosphere became locked away in the polar ice caps.

What might have caused this climate change is not known, though it may have been that the slow, processional movement of the planets through the solar system finally carried Mars too far from the sun. Caught in this change, a civilized race would have been forced to take drastic measures to avoid collapse or annihilation. A few may have escaped, fleeing inward to a warmer, wilder planet third from the sun. In doing so, they would have left their world dying, their cities crumbling—and on the surface of two dark moons, perhaps, some trace of their final passing.

★   ★   ★

The probe *Fobos 2*, in 1989, was clearly intended to search for evidence of anything odd or unnatural on the inner moon. Arguments stating otherwise are weakened by knowledge of the unusual planning that went into the project, and by the Russian predilection that Phobos is hollow.

Programmed to spend some two months maneuvering close to the Martian moon, the probe would have eventually conducted experiments from a distance of only 160 feet above the surface. It would also have dropped two modules to the surface. The modules were designed to study soil content, measure the magnetic field of Phobos, and relay panoramic views of the moon's surface. Afterward, *Fobos 2* was to return to Mars and begin a prolonged orbital study.

But of course none of this came to pass. After entering a temporary Mars orbit, *Fobos 2* transmitted images of the planet's surface.

It also sent back a good deal of data on the Martian environment. Then, on March 27, 1989, on schedule, it broke radio link with Kaliningrad in order to take photographs that would later assist mission planners in plotting a trajectory to Phobos. At the close of the photo session, the craft was programmed to turn its high-gain antenna back toward Earth. Instead, Kaliningrad received only a brief, weak signal, after which *Fobos 2* went silent, apparently forever.[22]

The photos sent back only deepened the mystery. One showed a system of straight lines about the planet's equator that look like cracks in dry earth.[23] However, since the camera was loaded with infrared film, scientists concluded that the lines were not a geological feature but were instead a vast source of heat. Each line was estimated to be about three to four kilometers wide. Another photo showed an oblong shadow, quite regular in its features, and quite large. However, the object casting the shadow—something obviously huge—was not visible in the photo.

The final photo, shown on the original *Sightings* series on the Fox television network, was a view not of Mars, but of something in space. The object in the photo appeared to be a dark, almost black, elongated streak. It has since become the subject of much debate. To some, it is merely a photographic glitch. To others, it is an alien probe. And to still others, it is a third (previously unknown) miniature moon in orbit around Mars.[24]

* * *

Photographs of the Red Planet taken by the two Viking orbiters in 1976 disclosed many startling Martian features, including some strongly suggestive of pyramids. From above, they look amazingly like our own terrestrial pyramids—an apex with four or more sloping sides. The official explanation for these formations is they are mountain peaks sculpted by powerful, aberrant air currents. Another strange feature is a vast belt of sand dunes encircling the

Martian north pole, which according to researchers may be the largest dune belt in the solar system.

More intriguing still is an enigma at the edge of one of the polar ice caps, dubbed "the searchlight" by NASA scientists. This is an area formed by "two diverging straight lines" between which the Martian surface is completely different from that of the surrounding terrain. So far, no one has offered a conclusive statement regarding the "searchlight." However, the man who was Viking orbiter imaging team leader, Michael H. Carr of the U. S. Geological Survey, made a statement at the time of discovery that "there appears to be some translucent cover over this region . . ."

★   ★   ★

Thirty-one months after the disappearance of *Fobos 2*, a strange object approached and passed within 288,000 miles of Earth. The object was first spotted with a small telescope on November 6, 1991, at Kitt Peak, Arizona. Believed to be an asteroid, continued observation revealed that it had a tendency to "wink"—that is, to become three times brighter, then dark again, every seven and one-half minutes. This led to speculation that the object was an artificial satellite, or even a spacecraft of some kind.

As the object continued to approach, astronomers at the European Southern Observatory in La Silla, Chile, tracked it with a sixty-inch telescope. Accurate measurements of the "winking" confirmed that the phenomenon was reminiscent of the pulsations of light observed on reflective, rapidly rotating satellites. The astronomers tracking the object were Richard West, Olivier Hainaut, and Alain Smette.

The mystery object came closest to Earth on December 5, 1991, after which it began drifting away. It was estimated to be about thirty feet in diameter. By the end of the month there were no further reports about the object.

* * *

Three days after the *Mars Observer* was scheduled to enter orbit, mission planners at JPL glumly concluded that the one billion dollar probe was gone, probably irretrievably lost.[25] Speculation abounded: the *Observer* was in orbit as planned, but was unable to contact Earth due to a faulty transistor in the craft's central clock. The probe failed to make orbit and went sailing off into interplanetary space. The oxygen/hydrazine propellant tanks ruptured during pressurization, destroying the craft.

Raised by observers outside the actual project, the explosion theory was frowned upon by JPL engineers. During a news conference at JPL, Glenn E. Cunningham, project director, said an explosion from overpressurization was highly unlikely due to various backup systems.[26] Sources outside said that although the probe was equipped with backup pressure regulators, the regulators would not have prevented a problem caused by an abrupt surge in pressure.

Meanwhile, fringe groups began announcing that the probe was still intact and transmitting on schedule. They claimed the transmitted data was being kept from the public because it revealed an alien presence on or around Mars.

Whatever the truth about the fate of the *Mars Observer*, there is no denying that—had it survived—the probe would have been able to locate and record evidence of intelligent life, past or present, on the Red Planet. An onboard camera designed by geologist Michael Malin, of Arizona State University, would have allowed astounding close-up photos of individual Martian features.[27] Costing thirteen million dollars, the camera was powerful enough so that it would have been able to obtain clear images of automobile-sized objects on the surface—objects such as the Viking landers sitting there since 1976, which NASA intended to photograph.

Other planned photos would have included close-ups of the famous "face" on Mars, located not far from the pyramids in the northern desert region known as Cydonia. Long regarded by geologists as nothing more than a curiosity of the Martian land-scape, the original *images* of the "face" bear a remarkable resemblance to a human visage peering skyward. I emphasize this statement because, popular opinion to the contrary, the "face" was photographed by *Viking* not just once, but twice; the photos were taken thirty-five days apart from different sun angles—one photo reinforcing the other.

☆ ☆ ☆

In early September 1993, only a week after the loss of the *Mars Observer*, the United States and Russia announced an "unprecedented" space exploration agreement.[28] Signed by then Vice President Al Gore and Prime Minister Victor Chernomyrdin, the agreement encouraged the pooling of technical and financial resources in matters of manned space exploration, including development and construction of the International Space Station, and future manned missions to the Moon, Mars, and beyond.

Three years after the agreement was signed, in August 1996, a team of scientists announced, during a carefully rehearsed NASA press conference, that they had found organic molecules—the carbon compounds that are the building blocks of life—in a small Martian meteorite. The potato-sized rock, discovered in Antarctica in 1984, also contained what appeared to be fossilized microbes. "The simplest explanation for these," said Dr. David McKay, of the Johnson Space Center in Houston and head of the research team, "is that they are the remains of Martian life."[29]

Then, three months later, on November 17, 1996, a Russian unmanned probe launched toward Mars failed to leave Earth orbit and plunged into the Pacific Ocean near Easter Island.[30] The cause of the crash was reported to be the failure of the fourth stage of the Russian Proton booster.

Less than eight months later, on July 4, 1997, a United States probe, *Pathfinder*, bounced to a landing on the Martian surface. *Pathfinder* was the first human device to successfully land on the

Red Planet since the days of Viking, more than two decades earlier. As it entered the atmosphere, the probe's descent was halted some fifty feet above the surface by parachute and retro-rocket. Huge balloons—inflated with explosive force—swathed *Pathfinder* in a protective cocoon. Then the parachute was cut loose. The probe plummeted the remaining distance to the surface and bounced repeatedly—as much as ten stories high with each bounce—before rolling to a halt. When the dust settled, the probe opened to release a small solar-powered dune buggy known as *Sojourner*.

For more than eighty days—until September 27, 1997, the date of its last successful transmission—the six-wheeled *Sojourner* roamed the Martian soil around *Pathfinder*, bumping into rocks and transmitting spectacular photos of an alien terrain. Meanwhile, *Pathfinder* verified that Mars was once warm, wet, and far more Earth-like than it is today.[31]

Even as *Pathfinder* and *Sojourner* transmitted information on soil/mineral composition and atmospheric conditions to Earth-side scientists, a second U.S. probe approached the Red Planet. This was *Mars Global Surveyor*, which entered orbit in mid-September 1997 and began systematically mapping and photographing the Martian surface. In April 1998, *Global Surveyor* transmitted photos of Cydonia, including an image of the enigmatic "face"—the first in over twenty years. Unfortunately, the new image was more akin to a shoe print than a face and seemed clearly natural in origin—a rocky butte or a mesa. When the photo was released over the Internet, conspiracy proponents immediately attacked NASA, insisting that the image was a forgery designed to hide the truth about intelligent life on Mars. Curiously enough, subsequent reports from NASA stated that the photo had indeed been filtered before being released, resulting in an image which, according to some astronomers, would be devoid of significant three-dimensional detail.

If nothing else, the controversy over the "face" serves to underscore the deepening mystery surrounding Mars, including the fate of the *Mars Observer* and earlier probes sent there. To date, one of

NASA's best explanations for the difficulties experienced on early missions is that the probes encountered a cloud of tiny particles, or space dust, which somehow affected the delicate trajectory and instrumentation of the craft. Unfortunately, the explanation seems lame, as does NASA's explanation for the disappearance of yet another Mars probe, the *Climate Orbiter*.

Like the *Mars Observer*, the $125 million *Climate Orbiter* vanished while entering orbit. On September 23, 1999, the probe successfully swung around to the far side of the Red Planet before all communication was lost. Project manager Richard Cook said the orbital insertion appeared to be at a far lower altitude then was considered safe: thirty-seven miles, or sixty kilometers, which means the *Orbiter* probably hit the atmosphere and broke up. The intended altitude was ninety-three miles (one-hundred and fifty kilometers), with a safe minimum altitude of fifty-three miles (eighty-five kilometers).

Several days after the *Orbiter's* disappearance, NASA announced that the probe was likely doomed by human error—in this case the failure to convert English units of measurement to metric units, causing a small but dire miscalculation in orbital approach. The explanation seemed plausible except for two things: (1) the *Orbiter* had traversed the entire 416 million miles to Mars without any hint of error, and (2) metric measurements (called newtons) are the accepted and recognized navigation standard on all such missions, making a conversion mistake unlikely. Had *Climate Orbiter* survived, it would have been able to take color photographs of Mars within a visual range that included both infrared and ultraviolet. By contrast, the already orbiting *Global Surveyor* can see only in black-and-white.

★ ★ ★

Whatever the truth about the various lost or malfunctioning probes, rest assured that robot emissaries will continue to travel to the Red Planet in order to pave the way for manned exploration. This will occur for a variety of reasons, the predominant one being the hope of finding life on Mars.

On December 3, 1999, the $165 million *Mars Polar Lander* arrived at the Red Planet carrying two microprobes. Designed to test for water and search for evidence of life near the Martian south pole, the Lander went silent after beginning its descent from orbit. Neither it, nor the microprobes—which were to have landed separately—have been heard from since.

Notes

1. John Noble Wilford, "Gloom is Growing Over the Outcome of a Mars Mission," *New York Times*, August 24, 1993, p. C5.

2. Wilford, "A Craft Nearing Mars Sends Back Only Silence, and Hope Dwindles," *New York Times*, August 25, 1993, p. AI 1.

3. Les Dorr, Jr., "Fobos Phlops," *Final Frontier*, August 1989, p. 7.

4. "The Great Galactic Ghoul," *Pursuit*, October 1972 [reprinted from *The National Observer*, November 13, 1971, "Mars and a Space Age Gremlin"], p. 80.

5. Ibid., p. 80.

6. Ibid, p. 80; also James E. Oberg, "The Great Galactic Ghoul," *Final Frontier*, October 1989, p. 10.

7. Carl Sagan, *The Cosmic Connection* (New York: Dell Publishing, 1973), p. 106.

8. Vyacheslav Kovtunenko, technical director, Russian Fobos project, "Next Stop Phobos," *Final Frontier*, April 1989, pp. 32, 36.

9. Carl Sagan, *The Cosmic Connection*, p. 106.

10. Sagan, astronomer and outspoken proponent of science, died of cancer on December 20, 1995. He was a skilled and convincing public speaker and perhaps the most famous scientist of this era, due largely to his ability to translate even the murkiest of scientific jargon into common language. In 1980, his PBS television series *Cosmos* attracted more Public Broadcast System viewers than any other show before it. His popularity and skill in utilizing the media set him at odds with key members of the

scientific community, who scorned Sagan by suggesting that his efforts to communicate publicly were unbecoming of a serious scientist.

11. Sagan, *The Cosmic Connection*, pp. 106–107.

12. Ibid, p. 107.

13. Ibid, pp. 108–109.

14. "Origin of the Grooves on Phobos," *Nature*, No. 273, pp. 282–284.

15. "Tidal Stresses Made Phobos Groovy," *New Scientist*, No. 74, p. 394.

16. Ibid, p. 394.

17. George H. Leonard, *Somebody Else is on the Moon* (David McKay Company, Inc., 1976).

18. Jonathan Swift, *Gulliver's Travels and Other Writings* (New York: Bantam Books, 1986) p. 168.

19. Robert J. Durant, "The Moons of Mars," *Pursuit*, January 1973, p. 11.

20. The map of Piri Ibn Haji Memmed. Piri was a Turkish admiral, a "re'is" in his own language, though the word is usually misspelled as "reis." His map was discovered in 1929 and a copy sent to President Wilson in 1930. A second copy was sent to the United States Navy Hydrographic Office in 1956. The map shows, in clear delineation, both the east and west coasts of South America, and yet it was drawn by Piri (or ordered drawn by him) only twenty years after Cristobal Colon (Christopher Columbus) made his first trip across the Atlantic. Piri Re'is claimed he copied the western coastline of South America from a map taken from a captured member of Colon's crew in 1513— the same year the explorer Balboa sailed into the Pacific! The source material for these maps—those in the possession of Colon and his men, and Piri's own—is thought to have been still earlier maps drawn during the twelfth and fourteenth centuries, found in Hebrew seminaries.

If this is true, Colon was almost certainly aware that new lands lay to the West. What makes these ancient maps so much the more astonishing is that they reveal certain aerial features of islands in the Arctic region—Ellesmere Island and other north-ern Canadian islands—which were completely unknown until the United States Air Force conducted a classified aerial survey in the 1950s. Moreover, they reveal a clearly delineated view of Queen Maud Land in the Antarctic region—a region apparently mapped before it became ice-covered. The topographical details of this area were only rediscovered somewhat recently, through seismological soundings of one and one-half-mile thick ice. A definitive history of the Piri Re'is map is contained in Professor Charles H. Hapgood's 1966 *Maps of the Ancient Sea Kings*. Inter-ested readers are also directed to the late Louis L'Amour's novel, *The Walking Drum*, which, though a fictional work, contains many carefully researched, nonfictional references to early Eastern cultures, especially Indian, Moslem, and Chinese, all of which are largely ignored by Western historians. L'Amour also refers repeatedly to the maps then possessed by sailors and navigators—maps ancient even in that day and age.

21. Sagan, *The Cosmic Connection*, pp. 133, 134.

22. Les Dorr, Jr., "Fobos Phlops," *Final Frontier*, August 1989, p. 7.

23. Geneva Hagen, "Martian Mystery Strikes Again" [Newswatch section], *Caveat Emptor*, Fall 1989, pp. 33–34.

24. Patrick Huyghe, "Martian Mystery: Is the Red Planet Host to a Third Lunar Body or UFOs?," *Omni* ("Antimatter" section), May 1993.

25. Wilford, "With *Observer* Silent, NASA Now Envisions 'Star Wars' Explorers of Mars," *New York Times*, August 27, 1993.

26. Wilford, "A Craft Nearing Mars Sends Back Only Silence," *New York Times*, August 25, 1993, pp. A1, A11.

27. Gary Taylor, "Fir$t Things Fir$t," *Final Frontier*, April 1989, pp. 12, 13.

28. Steven A. Holmes, "Russia, U.S. Sign Space, Energy Deal," *Patriot News*, Harrisburg, Pa. [*New York Times News Service*, September 2, 1993], p. A6.

29. Faye Flam, "Proof of Life on Mars? Some Scientists Cheer, and Some are Doubtful," *Philadelphia Inquirer*, August 8, 1996, pp. A1, A18; also, John Noble Wilford, "Replying to Skeptics, NASA Defends Claims About Mars," *New York Times*, August 8, 1996, pp. A1, D20.

30. Michael R. Gordon, "Russian Spacecraft Mystery: Where and How It Fell to Earth," *New York Times*, November 19, 1996, p. A13.

31. Paul Recer, "*Pathfinder* Detects Evidence of Mars-Earth Similarities," the Associated Press (*Patriot News*, Harrisburg, Pa.), December 5, 1997.

CHAPTER 10

Shapeshifters in the Sky

IN SEPTEMBER 1996, a woman residing in Central Scotland captured a remarkable image on video: a shape-changing UFO. The
incident occurred in Falkirk some twenty-five miles, or forty kilometers, west of Edinburgh, the capital. The witness, Margaret Ross,
told investigators she arose at daybreak (6:00 A.M.) on Friday, September 27, and saw a bright, pulsating object beyond her bedroom
window. As she watched, the object's perimeter "became pointed."[1]

Six months earlier a similar object had appeared in the Falkirk
sky, and Mrs. Ross had managed to videotape it before it vanished
from view. The tape was scrutinized at Glasgow University by a
retired professor of physics and astronomy, who deemed the object
unexplained. That object, however, was not as bright as the UFO
observed on September 27, which proved to be an even better
videotape subject.

For some forty minutes Mrs. Ross taped the UFO, which
appeared to pulsate while remaining otherwise motionless in the sky.
Then, abruptly, the object transformed into "a half-circle" and began

151

to rotate before returning to its original form. An instant later the object vanished—appearing to speed away to the east toward Linlithgow, a distance of ten kilometers or just over six miles.

Although Mrs. Ross didn't know it at the time, she was not the only witness. Two miles away, her daughter, Alexis, and son-in-law, George, and their two children also saw the shape-changing UFO. When Alexis telephoned her mother at about 7:00 A.M., she learned that Mrs. Ross had videotaped the object.

The tape was examined by UFO investigators, among them Ron Halliday of Stirling University, who declared it "one of the best [UFO] footages I have ever seen." Film of UFO phenomena is "very rare" and usually quite brief, Halliday observed, adding that there was no "obvious explanation" for the UFO image.[2]

Kenny Higgins, a long-time ufologist and chairman of Scottish Research Into Unidentified Flying Objects, seconded Halliday's opinion of the videotape. Higgins declared the videotape "as good a piece of evidence of a UFO in Scotland as I've ever seen."[3]

★ ★ ★

The ability to change shape, or appear to change shape, is an old—if somewhat uncommon—part of the UFO story. However, of late the shapeshift phenomenon has been observed far more frequently. Consider the following reports:

During the summer of 1995, a group of witnesses near Brighton Race Course in Sussex, England, reported seeing a white streak in the sky that changed into a triangular object, which then split into two spheres.[4] The sighting occurred at a time when the area was inundated with UFO activity.

In May 1996, a black boomerang-shaped object was reported circling over the town of Clayton, England. One of the witnesses, an unidentified woman, told investigators the object appeared to be solid, but that it also appeared to change shape as it moved. The UFO eventually disappeared into cloud cover.[5]

On February 22, 1997, at about 7:45 P.M., a Springfield, Oregon, couple videotaped a glowing, triangular-shaped UFO which became cylindrical in appearance before flashing away to the southeast.[6]

On August 19, 1997, at about 10:38 P.M., a mother and son were motoring to their home in Ipswich, England, when they spotted a gray saucer-shape over Bromeswell, near Woodbridge.[7] The pair had been visiting friends in Eyke, and before departing noticed that the television set was behaving oddly: the TV image would occasionally fade to a dark screen. The woman, who was driving, chose to follow the object in the hope of getting a better view. Her son later reported that the object changed from a saucer into a triangle of lights. The pair eventually lost sight of it in the vicinity of the Suffolk County Police headquarters.

These and similar shape-change accounts are anomalous even for researchers well versed in the bizarre. They raise difficult yet obvious questions: if UFOs are solid craft of some kind, how and (perhaps more importantly) *why* do they change shape, and why do they do this in front of witnesses? Can the objects change form and separate into different parts (as was reported at Brighton Race Course) and still adhere to the laws of classical mechanics? Or are they (as referred to in an earlier chapter) little more than holograms?

With these questions in mind, let's further complicate matters.

In September 1995, a newspaper in Wellington, England, published a letter describing an unusual aircraft sighted at Marshbrook, near Church Stretton.[8] The writer, identified hereafter as "WK," said the incident occurred in 1979 or 1980 while he and his wife were outside in an open field.

In his letter, WK said that a small jet aircraft passed overhead, flying normally but slowly. Then "a strange thing happened." The plane halted in midair and both he and his wife "heard the engine shut down." The plane remained motionless for about a minute before the engine restarted, and then it flew off.

Expressing bewilderment over the incident, WK noted that a midair halt and engine shutdown is of course impossible for any conventional jet aircraft. An expert in aircraft recognition, he said he was unable to identify the plane, which he described as similar to the Jet Provost then in use by the British Royal Air Force, though "slightly different in size and outline, like, say, *a copy made from a drawing* [emphasis added]." He said the aircraft was not a Harrier—a British vertical takeoff jet in service since the late 1960s. In fact, he said he had a "nagging doubt" about whether it was an airplane at all: "Was it," he asked, "a UFO?"

If, in asking this, WK actually meant "Was the object a space-craft?" then the answer is almost certainly no, it was not. At the same time, however, his experience is not without precedent. Similar tales of "ghost aircraft" have been documented since at least the 1950s, and when one compares the reports and recognizes the remarkable and unconventional behavior attributed to the objects, there remains little doubt that these sightings are a part of the UFO experience.

Consider the following summary, extracted from the U.S. Air Force Project Blue Book Special Report No. 14:

> A naval aviation student, his wife, and several others were at a drive-in movie from 21:15 to 22:40 hours [9:15 P.M. to 10:40 P.M.] on April 20, 1952, during which time they saw several groups of objects fly over. There were from two to nine objects in a group and there were about twenty groups. The groups of objects flew in a straight line except for some changes in direction accomplished in a manner like any standard aircraft turn.
>
> The objects were shaped like conventional aircraft. The unaccountable feature . . . was that each had a red glow surrounding it and it [the object] was glowing itself, although it was a cloudless night.

The above sighting was one of only twelve of an original 434 "unknowns" identified in Special Report 14 as "good" unknowns.

Each had to fit certain criteria involving physical description, aerial maneuvers, and background data in order to make the cut.

* * *

In early 1971, residents of the Middletown, Ohio, area were treated to another version of the phantom airplane phenomenon. The incident received almost no attention from the mainstream media, but was described in full by B. Roman, editor of the defunct *Ohio UFO Reporter*. She recounted the incident as follows:[9]

> It was after 11:00 P.M. Monday, January 18 [1971], when calls began coming in to WPFB Radio about a large aircraft circling over the trailer park next to Lesourdsville Lake, near Middletown on Route 4. One lady said she had been watching it circle for more than forty-five minutes, that it had a loud motor and flashing lights. Another caller said it had landed, and the highway patrol had gone to investigate; still another said it had left the area briefly but had returned.
>
> During this time, numerous local citizens band radio operators were beginning to [report] that they were seeing the plane. One, a resident of the trailer park, said he had been watching it for some time, that it was constantly flying a circular pattern over the park at an altitude of 800 to 1,000 feet.
>
> Another, a pilot, said he'd just heard over his radio that the FAA had sent a plane to investigate but failed to establish contact. Callers to the airport and police were informed that [the aircraft] was apparently [flown by] a pilot who had radio trouble. A member of the local Civil Defense patrol telephoned me [Roman] to say that he had been in touch with Wright-Patterson AFB in Dayton, Ohio. To his knowledge the FAA had not been called in.
>
> At this point several friends arrived and we drove to Lesourdsville Lake. As we approached, we could see a large craft circling slowly at about 800 feet, as reported.

We stopped the car and I got out, but could hear nothing. The craft had several flashing red lights and gave the appearance of flying at a forty-five degree angle at all times.

Then a smaller craft with a loud motor came into the area. It looked like a white light, stopping at times, and growing larger as it neared the first plane. Both continued circling for some time—at one point we thought they were going to collide head-on. Then the plane with the flashing red lights headed east-northeast; the second one with the large white light followed briefly, then went north-northeast. As it [the second object] passed overhead, we could see a beam projecting ahead of the light.

The craft with the flashing red lights apparently continued northeast. CB'ers there were telling others that it was circling their area and that it had a loud motor, which made things vibrate as it passed over quite low. . . .

Later [the next day, January 19], a resident of South Middletown said that, before the appearance of the plane, he'd seen a helicopter go over which made a strange "humming" sound.

One other detail should be noted here. According to Roman, members of the Civil Air Patrol identified the mystery airplane as a C-119 "Flying Boxcar."

Was a Flying Boxcar maneuvering in the dark Ohio skies during January 1971? If so, the aircraft was in violation of federal aviation regulations by circling low over homes. And what of the other object, which approached and for a time followed the larger aircraft? Was it in some way related to the report of a "humming" helicopter?

During the 1960s and 1970s, John Keel found that the C-119 "boxcar" configuration was often observed in UFO flap areas. In his book *Operation Trojan Horse*, he reported that "for a long time I suspected that the Air Force was sending special instrument-laden planes into flap areas to take photographs and perform various tests. But eventually the circumstantial evidence mounted, and I had to discard this plausible theory for an implausible one, i.e., that aircraft *resembling* C-119s were being deployed in flap sectors, but they weren't related to the Air Force."[10]

In more recent years there have been fewer reports of strange military cargo aircraft in sighting areas, though such tales continue to be heard. The following account, passed along by Rick Hilberg, was originally documented by reporter Paul Adams of the *Faribault* (Minnesota) *Daily News*.

On April 2, 1991, a theater owner in Faribault spotted an odd-looking object in the sky while driving to work. The time was about 7:00 P.M. He described the object as white in color and oblong, and said it was suspended vertically in the sky like a hot-air or a helium-filled balloon. Later, while returning home, he again saw the object, only now it appeared to be red and green in color. Arriving home, he summoned his wife, children, and neighbors to watch the object.

A small crowd gathered, but abruptly two large aircraft arrived and diverted everyone's attention from the UFO. The planes came in low and at a reduced speed—so low, in fact, that one resident later said he thought they were going to land on his house. The planes were quite close—virtually "nose to tail," a dangerous and idiotic maneuver especially when flying over a residential area.

As the aircraft flew overhead, someone in the crowd waved and one of the planes briefly turned on a bank of floodlights. Later, other aircraft arrived and a total of eleven planes were counted, along with a number of helicopters. Eventually all the aircraft departed. The UFO itself disappeared during the confusion.

A spokesman for the Minnesota Air National Guard told reporters that two C-130 military transports were conducting maneuvers in the Faribault area that night. However, the spokesman claimed that no other military aircraft were in the area, and he said that none of the C-130 crewmen reported seeing any strange objects in the sky. There was no explanation for why the C-130s (if in fact that's what they were) were flying "nose-to-tail" above a residential area.

Inquiries with the National Weather Service ruled out the possibility that the UFO was a weather balloon, as none had been released in the area.

★ ★ ★

During the spring of 1968, two students of East Texas State University, Gary Massey and Richard Shumer, were driving along State Highway 11, five miles east of Commerce, Texas. Suddenly, approaching from the west, they saw a strange flying object: a plane "reminiscent of a B-29 bomber" with wings shorter and thicker than ordinary aircraft wings, but with no cockpit, no pilot's cabin or windows, no propellers, no apparent exhaust or contrail, and "no sound whatsoever" even though the craft passed almost directly over the witnesses and at a relatively low altitude and slow speed.[11] The strange craft was a "nondescript" brown or gray in color.

A report on the sighting was compiled by anomalist Tom Adams, who noted that although the mystery aircraft was moving in a westerly direction when first observed, it quickly changed direction and began moving east, parallel to the car. The aircraft then changed direction again, moving south and at right angles to the witnesses' automobile.

By this time the car had been halted and the two men were standing on the shoulder of the road. They saw no external markings, insignia, or identification of any sort, even though the plane passed overhead at no more than 200 to 300 feet. Massey later commented that the object looked like "a *dummy or mock-up airplane* [emphasis added]."

★ ★ ★

On the early morning of Sunday, September 12, 1993, in the town of Tavistock, England, a commotion arose in the car park outside the Spring Hill Hostel and Flats. Located in the county of Devon, Tavistock is about fifty miles west-southwest of the port city of

Exmouth, and south of Dartmoor National Park. The park, spanning some 365 square miles (950 square kilometers), is known for its trout streams, peat bogs, and howling winds, and recalls to mind the "melancholy moor" described by Arthur Conan Doyle in his *Hound of the Baskervilles.*

At about 12:35 A.M., individuals in the car park noticed an arrangement of lights in the sky approaching from the direction of Plymouth Road. As the lights drew near they illuminated an object which, according to one person, was about as large as a "medium-sized aeroplane."[12]

The witness said the object had a catamaran-like twin fuselage and "two rows of cabin windows." It had no wings. He estimated the object's altitude at about 1,500 to 2,000 feet, and said it remained in view for about a minute and was absolutely silent. The object followed the main street north toward Dartmoor National Park and the town of Okehampton beyond.

Despite the object's strange appearance, not everyone that night was convinced that what they saw was anything other than an oddly designed airplane. But according to the aforementioned eyewitness, anyone at the scene could attest that it made no sound. Acting on the possibility that the UFO was a plane, the witness said he checked with British Airways and discovered that there were no commercial flights at that hour. He also learned that no military flights had been reported in the area that Sunday morning.

★　★　★

On February 28, 1971, Michael Jaffe, founder of a UFO amateur radio network known as Data-Net, was motorcycling along California Highway 17 in the southern portion of the state, just south of the town of Hayward.[13] A careful observer and a pioneer in the field of ufology, Jaffe was witness to an intriguing event, later recounted in the publication *Flying Saucer Review*, "Case Histories, Supplement No. 5."

Cycling through moderately heavy traffic, Jaffe noticed two sailplanes being towed aloft. Quite unexpectedly, he saw something else in the sky: a bizarre glowing object pursued by a twin-engine aircraft "smaller than a C-25." Because of the heavy traffic and the wind, "I was able to watch this scene for no more than about four seconds," Jaffe explained. "The object appeared to be two brilliant spheres, each about twelve inches wide and about twelve inches apart, but with a hazy connection or 'link' between them and also trailing behind the spheres." Jaffe said that the leading sphere was a brilliant red in color, while the trailing globe was a brilliant blue. Its altitude was roughly one hundred yards.

Whether the pursuing aircraft was in some way directly associated with the UFO remains impossible to say, since, according to Jaffe, the plane seemed quite conventional. Nevertheless, its proximity to the UFO—the fact that the two objects appeared to be pacing one another—is in itself curious. On the other hand, reports of aircraft pacing or escorting UFOs are not as unique as one might expect.

On Sunday, March 16, 1997, a resident of Blowing Rock, North Carolina, telephoned the local newspaper to ask if anyone had reported seeing a luminous flying disc. The caller said she had spotted the object at about 11:00 A.M. while looking out the glass doors of her living room, fronting onto the Pisgah National Forest. Other individuals at various locations also reported seeing the UFO.[14]

The strangest thing about the sighting, the witness said, was that the disc was being escorted—at a somewhat leisurely pace—by three jets, which appeared to be military aircraft! She said the jets were slightly smaller than the UFO, with one positioned behind and two below.

* * *

On October 11, 1966, a brilliant aerial light "as big as a car" visited the Wanaque Reservoir in New Jersey. The object, observed by Sgt. Ben Thompson of the Pompton Lakes Police Department, did typical UFO maneuvers, including making right-angle turns at impossible speeds. After the object had departed, the airplanes and helicopters arrived.

"There were seven helicopters and, I would say, ten or twelve jets," Thompson told investigators. "I've never seen seven helicopters in this area in all my life—and I've lived here for forty years."15

Unmarked helicopters have been showing up in UFO flap areas and at animal mutilation sites since the mid-1960s. The presence of helicopters in mutilation areas has given rise to the suspicion that the government or military is somehow involved in the slaughter. Whether or not this is true, the problem remains serious for farmers, ranchers, and law enforcement personnel throughout the United States as well as in various other parts of the world.

In the Winter 1977 issue of *Pursuit*, executive editor R. Martin Wolf reported on the apparent link between unexplained animal deaths and the mystery helicopters. Wolf's observations, part of a lengthy article, were based on a firsthand look at the UAD phenomenon with partner Steve Mayne. Wolf wrote:

> Many accounts of "black helicopters" and "UFOs" are reported to sheriff's departments in counties where mutilations are occurring . . . We took a photograph of one of these. This one was strange only in its actions (it veered away when we filmed it) and by the fact that when questioned, no agency in the area would claim it as their own, nor were there any records of its presence in the area.
>
> A sheriff in Colorado told us that one evening [during a period of continued mutilations in his county] he was driving on the ground while his deputy flew a light airplane over an area where mutilations had occurred in the past, when they were notified by the Air Force that there was a helicopter fifty feet below the deputy's plane. For the two hours that the sheriff and the deputy chased the "helicopter," it remained on radar—sometimes in

front of the plane, sometimes behind it, occasionally over or under it; but neither the deputy in the air nor the sheriff in his car on the ground could see it. "There was simply nothing there." It didn't go away. The sheriff and his deputy, running low on fuel and high on frustration, gave up and went home after two hours.[16]

Where do you draw the line; what constitutes reality? When is a helicopter *not* a helicopter?

★ ★ ★

At about midnight on August 21, 1975, law enforcement officials in Kimball County, Nebraska, responded to the presence of a low-flying aircraft. The object, detected briefly on radar by Air Force personnel at Cheyenne, Wyoming, was winging across the Wyoming-Nebraska border at the ridiculous altitude of 100 to 150 feet.[17]

For nearly five hours a chase continued until finally, about ten miles from Bushnell, Nebraska, the law closed to within a half-mile of the mysterious craft, which proved to be—what else?—a helicopter. At one point in the chase, the chopper hovered briefly over a Strategic Air Command missile silo located just south of Bushnell. Shortly afterward, it vanished to the south in the direction of the Colorado border.

By the end of 1975, helicopter hysteria was reaching record highs in the southwest, as documented in the November 13, 1975 edition of the *Denver Record Stockman*. According to writer Pat Kalahar, from two to seven "ghost copters" were reported that week in the New Mexico counties of Quay and Union, with more than thirty additional reports during the previous month. Cattle mutilations were numerous at the time, and several congressmen and the Federal Aviation Administration became involved, but no answers were forthcoming.

Two decades later, the phantom helicopter aviators were still at it. A March 1996 story in the *Casper* (Wyoming) *Star-Tribune* reported that for more than a year an "unknown force" had been flying formations of helicopters several nights a week near Casper Mountain.[18] The FAA and the Army National Guard were at a loss to explain the activity, routinely observed by control tower personnel at Natrona County International Airport. The newspaper quoted an FAA memo, which stated that tower personnel had "observed, on numerous occasions, what appears to be slow moving aircraft along the north side of Casper Mountain," often as many as fourteen at a time. According to the memo, the aircraft were thought to be helicopters. Ground observers, meanwhile, reported watching the strobe lights of helicopters through night-vision glasses, and one man even claimed to have discovered a parked black helicopter on the mountaintop; he said he scraped paint from its side while evading black-garbed soldiers, and said he had the paint analyzed—claiming it was a military style, anti-radar coating.

Mystery helicopters were numerous both in the British Isles and in the United States during the fall of 1998.

On the night of Thursday, October 8, 1998, UFO sightings were accompanied by helicopter activity in the vicinity of Swansea, on the coast of South Wales.[19] Among the witnesses was UFO investigator Neil Spring, who described seeing a "pencil-shaped" object illuminated by two "fiery red" lights. Spring also reported seeing three helicopters, one of which pursued the UFO but failed to catch it. Newspaper reports later confirmed that military helicopters had landed at Swansea Airport on the night of October 8. However, airport personnel downplayed the UFO reports, saying the objects were probably RAF Sea King helicopters conducting night maneuvers.

In Arkansas the following week, law enforcement officials received numerous reports of unmarked helicopters in Baxter, Boone, and Newton counties.[20] One report—made by a lawman in Baxter County—described two dark green helicopters flying below 500 feet. The sighting occurred on October 14 at 9:00 P.M. Inquiries by members of the Arkansas State Police and the Army National Guard failed to determine the origin of the helicopters.

* * *

During the winter of 1975–76, a series of bizarre helicopter events took place in New England. Details were passed along by ufologist Betty Hill, and are summarized as follows:

> In mid-December 1975, a woman living in Rye Beach, New Hampshire awoke one morning at 4:00 A.M. to find her bedroom illuminated "as though it were daytime." As she nervously lit a cigarette, the room suddenly went dark. According to Betty Hill, "for the next three weeks, the woman was awakened between 3:00 and 4:00 A.M. by the sound of helicopters above the salt marshes in front of her home."

> On December 21, 1975, an unidentified aerial object followed the same woman—who was returning home late at night—for a distance of about fifteen miles. The object hovered nearby while she ran from the car to the house. It left soon thereafter.

> During the week of February 20, 1976, a farmer reported an increase in helicopter activity around her home near Wells, Maine. At one point, she watched "two helicopters side-by-side over the highway, at night, during a severe snowstorm. They looked as though they were refueling in midair as she could see a connection [joining] one to the other." The woman also reported that the choppers were silent: she was unable to hear any engine sound.[21]

Before going any further, I should note that it would be suicidal to fly helicopters side-by-side in a snowstorm as described. Even in the best of weather, chopper pilots are careful about flying in proximity because of the resulting blade turbulence. What's more, I've heard of only a few helicopters outfitted for aerial refueling from fixed-wing aircraft and none, to my knowledge, from other helicopters.

On the night of December 8, 1975, Betty Hill had her own experience with a phantom helicopter. She reported that while driving home she found herself being followed by "two rows of puzzling lights in the sky." The pattern consisted of "four red lights on the right and four green lights on the left, which formed a V." She further related: "As I turned into my driveway, I discovered that it [the illuminated object] was a helicopter. It flew low over my car and garage, and barely missed the tree in my backyard. There was one large white light on the front of the craft, but none on the tail. It disappeared swiftly from sight."

★   ★   ★

On the night of October 5, 1973, a woman and two boys confronted the unknown over Keats Island near Vancouver, British Columbia. They were on a UFO watch (sightings were numerous at the time) when they were overflown by an object that looked and sounded like a prop-driven airplane.[22] The plane maneuvered over the trio, then turned and flew back the way it had come. After going only a short distance the aircraft suddenly stopped *and hovered, and all sound ceased.* At the same time, the navigational lights on the plane "blinked out" and were replaced by a string of six horizontal lights. The object hovered for several minutes before vanishing from view.

That same night, on Vancouver Island some fifty miles away, members of the Quamichan Indian tribe were at their fishing camp along the Cowichan River, when they spotted something extremely odd in the sky only a few hundred feet away.[23] "It didn't make any sound and it was something we had never seen before," one of the witnesses was quoted in the *Canadian UFO Report.*

The object, a flying disc, had "three red lights rotating around the top part" and "blinking lights going in the opposite direction around the middle part. There was another light at the very top—a red flashing one. Then, from the bottom, a white beam shone out like a spotlight. The beam moved up the river as if it [the UFO] was looking for something. By this time we were all pretty scared."

What happened next was even more frightening.

"If we told people about this, they'd think we were crazy," the witness confided. "But all of a sudden it looked as if it [the disc] had turned into an airplane! It made a noise like a plane and it looked like a plane, and all the lights went out except for a little red one. It went right past us and disappeared over the trees."

★   ★   ★

There it is. Two separate incidents on the same night, in the same geographical area, each the opposite of the other but each one clearly demonstrating that UFOs and ghost aircraft are—on occasion if not always—one and the same.

What, then, do we make of this? If UFOs are in fact spacecraft, as so many believe, do we explain the shape-change phenomenon as a kind of chameleon technology—a means by which the crew is able to alter the spacecraft's external appearance? If so, and the intent is to conceal the spacecraft to avoid detection, what purpose is served by using this technology in full view of witnesses? What's more, shape-change reports, as noted earlier, seem to be growing in number. Peter Davenport, director of the National UFO Reporting Center in Seattle, said in January 2001 that the shape-change phenomenon is "something we do not understand, but it is reported to us frequently."[24]

Commenting further, Davenport said the increased number of shape-change reports could be related to heightened media exposure and public awareness. He said an increase in radio interviews and news stories has made both him and the center better known, resulting in a corresponding increase in quality reports.

Speculating on the possible cause of the shape-change phenomenon, the director said an observer might be fooled into believing a UFO had changed form if the object was moving or changing position rapidly. He said the movement could alter the witness perspective, resulting in the illusion of shape-change.

For anyone who has ever been fooled by an airplane appearing to change shape as it turned or maneuvered in flight, and in light of the widespread belief that UFOs are an alien technology, i.e., interstellar craft, transdimensional craft, or the like, Davenport's explanation is clearly plausible. However, the bulk of the shape-change documentation presented here suggests that something different is frequently at work, something "alien" but not extraterrestrial.

There are a number of alternative explanations that could be examined closely at this point, but allow me to summarize a few of the more relevant UFO theories. One view is that the UFO phenomenon represents a form of manifested consciousness—an intelligence apart from human mind and thought that has coexisted with us through the ages and communicates in mythic form . . . appearing before witnesses as gods, fairies, creatures of various shape and form, and of course space aliens. Another is that UFOs are a kind of visionary experience, more akin to dream than reality, though real enough to be interpreted as an actual event. The idea here is that such an occurrence would be shaped by the psychological and social environment of the observer, hence this view is referred to as the "psychosocial" hypothesis.* A third view is the "paraphysical" theory—the belief that the subconscious mind helps shape reality by introducing a short-lived but nonetheless tangible anomaly (a UFO or some other aberration) into the conscious environment. This view, once widely embraced and emphasizing a psychic component to the UFO phenomenon, has fallen into disrepute in recent years.

When it comes to the nature and origin of UFOs there is, however, one undeniable truth that stands above all the theories. This truth is that regardless of what we wish to believe, we are still all just guessing. We really do not know what UFOs are, where they come from, or why some of them appear to change shape or

---

* One problem with this hypothesis is the existence of apparently genuine UFO photos and videotape. Can a dream or a vision be photographed?

James W. Moseley addressing enthusiasts at the 1994 National UFO Conference, held that year in Cleveland. He believes the UFO phenomenon is "interrelated to the most fundemental mysteries of human life . . ." (Photo by Benita C. Owens from the R. Hilberg collection)

indeed do any of the amazing things they have been reported doing. And because we don't know, we sift the meager available data; we theorize and surmise, and in the process we sometimes disregard information that runs contrary to our own ideas. In short, we jump to conclusions. We take a position, we challenge, we argue, we defend. And somewhere in the midst of it all we find that we have been considering circumstances and possibilities that would otherwise be completely foreign to our way of thinking.

This is what the UFO phenomenon does to us: unless we are obtuse or extremely frightened, it forces us to think in a deeper, more meaningful way.

Dr. Leo Sprinkle, a retired professor of psychology at Wyoming University, once said that he believes UFO activity "is part of a larger educational program."[25] Long-time anomalist Floyd Murray has said that UFOs seem to be "guideposts telling us where to go next. . . . Something, somewhere, wants to direct our attention upwards or inwards, wants us to start thinking about our origins, our universe . . ."[26] In a moment of personal revelation, James Moseley once declared that he believes the UFO phenomenon to be "interrelated [to] the most fundamental mysteries of human life: Where did we come from, why are we here, where (if anywhere) do we go next?"[27] Others studying the UFO mystery have made similar observations.

I believe this is the ultimate point of the UFO experience. The mystery is not about extraterrestrial life or interdimensional visitors (although they are certainly something to think about). It is about us. It has always been about us! We are students in a cosmic classroom and we are being teased, tricked, and manipulated into a greater awareness. In the end, we may discover that our world—our reality—is not what it seems, not at all what we suspect from our current grasp of science and nature. We may find that our universe, and all it contains, is little more than a reflection of our own ever-changing thoughts, beliefs, and dreams.

Notes

1. "Unidentified Light in the Sky Taped," *Courier & Advertiser*, Dundee, Scotland, October 14, 1996.

2. Ibid.

3. Ibid.

4. Richard Worley, "The Sussex Files," *Brighton & Hove Leader*, Sussex, England, July 3, 1997.

5. "UFO Watchers Spot 'Boomerang' Object," *Evening Sentinel*, Stoke-On-Trent, England, May 20, 1996.

6. Joe Mosley, "Camera Helps to Catch Strange Lights in the Sky," *Register-Guard*, Eugene, Oregon, February 28, 1997.

7. "Mum and Son Chase UFO in Car," *Evening Star*, Ipswich, England, August 21, 1997.

8. "Was It a UFO?", letter published September 11, 1995 in the *Shropshire Star*, Wellington, England.

9. Curt Sutherly and David Fideler, "The Phantom Starships," *UFO Report*, May 1978, pp. 16–18.

10. John A. Keel, *UFOs: Operation Trojan Horse* (New York, G. P. Putnam's Sons, 1970), pp. 125–126.

11. Sutherly and Fideler, "The Phantom Starships," pp. 18–19.

12. "Strange, Silent Craft Sighted Flying Across the Night Sky," *Tavistock Times Gazette*, Devon, England, September 16, 1993.

13. Sutherly and Fideler, "Phantom Starships," p. 19.

14. Jennifer Bent, "UFO Over Blowing Rock," *Watauga Democrat*, Boone, North Carolina, March 21, 1997.

15. Sutherly and Fideler, "Phantom Starships," p. 19.

16. R. Martin Wolf, "Chaos in Quiesence," *Pursuit* (Vol. 10, No. 1), Winter 1977, p. 26.

17. Sutherly and Fideler, "The Phantom Starships," p. 19.

18. Jason Marsden and Deirdre Stoelzle, "Strange Lights in Sky Over Casper," *Star-Tribune*, Casper, Wyoming, March 21, 1996.

19. Chris Peregrine, "X-Files UFO Riddle in City," and Rhodri Evans, "UFO Mystery is Deepening," *South Wales Evening Post*, October 9 and October 12, 1998 respectively.

20. "Mystery Choppers Fly Low Over Area," *Baxter Bulletin*, Mountain Home, Arkansas, October 15, 1998.

21. Personal correspondence with Betty Hill, 1976, 1977.

22. Sutherly and Fideler, "The Phantom Starships," p. 79.

23. Ibid., p. 79.

24. January 8, 2001 telephone interview with Peter Davenport.

25. Zack Van Eyck, "Abductees Aren't as Alone as They Think," *Desert News*, Salt Lake City, Utah, June 30, 1996.

26. Floyd Murray, "UFO Research: Some Thoughts on the State of the Art," *Caveat Emptor* (No. 16), Winter 1988–89, p. 18.

27. James W. Moseley, "Forty Years in Ufology," *Saucer Smear* (Vol. 40, No. 1), January 10, 1993, pp. 2, 3.

Ufology serves as a social gathering point for the scattered participants in a brilliant and classical bohemian subculture, as well as a vehicle for the exploration of the unknown.

. —Allen H. Greenfield

A Gathering

THE ARIZONA SUN was hot, the temperature over one hundred degrees, and I luxuriated in the absence of humidity.

A mile away, the Superstition Mountains rose at the end of a long, hard-packed dirt road. They stood tall and angular, unlike the ancient, worn Appalachians of my native Pennsylvania. I shifted position, focused my camera and shot several frames. Then I turned and hiked back to where I had parked the rental car.

I was in Arizona on vacation. I was also there to attend a gathering of UFO investigators and enthusiasts, the 26th Annual National UFO & New Age Conference.

My plan had been to arrive in Phoenix, the conference site, two days early. I would tour the old Apache Trail (U.S. 88) one day and run south to Nogales, Mexico, the next. An airline cancellation put me in Phoenix much later than expected; I was forced to postpone my visit to Mexico. I did spend a full day following the Apache Trail—stopping frequently to hike in the desert, and grabbing a

171

burger and beer in tiny Tortilla Flat (pop. 6). By day's end I was back in Phoenix, and the next day the conference began.

My recollection of the conference, held in September 1989, is included here as a personal account of the people, the mood, and one or two rather unusual experiences.

Thursday night, September 14, I was enjoying dinner alone in the restaurant of the Quality Inn West, the site of the conference. Occasionally, as I dined, a young woman working in the adjacent lounge would walk through the dining room on the way to the kitchen. Each time she opened the heavy lounge door a roar of conversation could be heard. Finishing my meal, I asked the girl—her name was Linda—if the noise was being caused by persons registered for the conference. She said it was, and added that her lounge was "usually not this noisy."

Walking around to the main entrance, I was able to look in and study the crowd without being seen. Seated at a table was James Moseley, one of the key figures in ufology and a man who could easily be described as a "godfather" in the field. In 1967, in New York City, Moseley promoted the first large-scale UFO convention. The event—held during the weekend of June 24 (the twentieth anniversary of Kenneth Arnold's sighting)—attracted literally thousands of individuals and set a standard that has yet to be equaled for attendance or audacity.[1] At the time, Moseley published a widely read UFO magazine, *Saucer News*. He eventually dropped the magazine format and resurrected the publication as *Saucer Smear*—an irreverent, opinionated UFO newsletter.

Surrounding Moseley at the lounge table were several people, some familiar, some not. Tim Beckley—conference co-host and publisher of New Age and UFO books—was on his feet, moving restlessly around the room.[2] Though we had never met, I recognized him from published photos. Also present was J. Antonio Huneeus, another man I had never met. Antonio divides his time between writing activities in New York City and UFO research in his native Chile. Seated opposite Moseley was a face not immediately identifiable, though familiar. It turned out to be Edward

Moseley and Allan J. Manak at the 1994 National UFO Conference. Manak was a member of the permanent organizing
committee of the NUFOC, of which Moseley is chairman.
(Photo by Benita C. Owens from the R. Hilberg collection)

Biebel, formerly of Cleveland and at the time living in Nogales,
Arizona. Ed was a longtime ufologist and a professional photographer. Still another at the table was co-host Jim Speiser, founder and
former director of ParaNet, a UFO computer information service.

Watching Moseley from across the lounge, I recalled my first
contact with the man in more than a decade. A year earlier I had
written to Jim at the urging of UFO researcher Floyd Murray. In my
letter, I asked to be added to his *Saucer Smear* mailing list. Moseley
quickly responded—dubbing me "Agent Orange" in his reply. It was
a joke based on the paranoia that has always clouded the UFO field.
Everyone suspects everyone else of being a government spy. I currently work for the government, though in a rather lowly position
and not, of course, as a spy, but Jim couldn't resist the inference.

I turned it around on him when I walked into the lounge. "Sir,"
I said, looking directly at Moseley. "Agent Orange, reporting as
ordered."

The conversation at the table fell off noticeably. Moseley sat there, his mouth gaping. He stared at me. Then he looked around at everyone else. "Who is this guy?" he finally asked. No one replied. "Does anyone know who he is?"

No one did. I had changed in twelve years. Finally, I identified myself, but Jim didn't understand the Agent Orange reference. I reminded him about his note. He didn't remember.

A moment later I was seated with the group, sparring verbally with Moseley and Biebel. The banter was good-natured and jovial. Watching Beckley, I sensed his preoccupation, his need to make the conference a success. Speiser, on the other hand, impressed me with his relaxed, quiet attitude—though he missed little of what went on around him. At one point I looked up as the author Brad Steiger entered the lounge. I rose and introduced myself. Someone else—Moseley, I think—muttered "Broad Stagger" (recalling a published article satirizing the man).

Brad and I corresponded during the 1970s, but we had never previously met. He remembered my name and accepted a handshake. He had a strong grip, an easy smile, and radiated tremendous good will.

The conversation continued into the wee hours. Finally, Linda threw us out of the lounge.

★　★　★

Despite the late night, I was up early the following morning. I exercised and showered, and was off to the restaurant for breakfast. There I was hailed from a side table where Ed Biebel was seated with several others.

The breakfast conversation focused in part on UFO matters, though none of it seriously. In fact, the previous night's conversation had waxed serious only once: that was when Brad, Ed, and I touched on some unpleasant moments in the field—events that included, for each of us, strange and sometimes frightening phone calls or telephonic interference, or phenomena such as the auto-

At Mysticon—a combined UFO/science-fiction convention in Cleveland in 1975. The author, second from right flanked on the right by ufologist Robert Easley and (at far left) magazine publisher Eugene Steinberg and Rick Hilberg. (Photo by Allen Greenfield from the R. Hilberg collection)

mobile headlight problem described in the Preface. Such phenomena are an intrinsic part of the UFO experience. They generate fear and paranoia, and serve only to intensify any involvement with the unknown.

Later that morning, a press conference was held to preview scheduled talks. Unfortunately, most speakers didn't know when to stop. Instead of whetting the media appetite, they killed it. The one camera crew present packed up long before the list of speakers was exhausted.

Eugene Steinberg made his first weekend appearance during the press gathering. I have known Gene for many years. A sometime publisher, he was pivotal in my development as a writer. In the early 1970s, while working as a professional radio newsman, he launched a magazine called *Caveat Emptor*, focusing on reports of UFOs and unexplained phenomena.[3] Floyd Murray and I became two of Gene's regular contributors. We were both novices—

"wannabes" in the world of journalism. Gene gave each of us a voice in his magazine.

Gene and I had last been at a convention together fourteen years earlier, in October 1975, at the Trade Winds Inn, Fort Smith, Arkansas. The event was billed as the first International UFO Conference and attracted a plethora of players, including a large number of scientists and engineers as well as representatives of every large UFO research group. It was supposed to be a program "united for objectivity," but tension and antagonism were evident throughout—so much so that physicist Stanton Friedman, a guest speaker and no stranger to the controversy that abounds in UFO circles, declared of the group hostilities: "A pox on all their houses if they wish to fight with one another."

Indeed, those who had paid admission to hear about the UFO phenomenon found the atmosphere repellent. Allen Greenfield of Atlanta, Georgia, one of the brightest thinkers in the field, summed up the disgust many felt for the petty rivalry: "I'm picking up vibes of discontent from all over," he said. "They're getting sick of it."

Like many UFO conventions, the Fort Smith conference was more of a reunion of old friends and enemies than a platform for scientific endeavor. That it succeeded in attracting a number of scientists was a step in the right direction. But Gene and I were there to enjoy and to record the proceedings for later publication, and we did, though sometimes we too got caught in the arguments.

Gene was vacationing with his wife and son in nearby Scottsdale at the time of the 1989 Phoenix gathering. Because of this, he found himself traveling to and from, dividing his time between family and conference. Subsequently, he missed a few of the more unusual events, none of which were on any scheduled agenda.

* * *

For reasons not at all hard to understand, a substantial amount of shop talk (read: gossip) took place in the lounge of the Quality Inn. I entered that place Friday night to discover ufologist

Look, up in the sky! Mysticon in 1976. From left, Carol Hilberg, Eugene Steinberg, Robert Easley, and Rick Hilberg. (Photo by Allen Greenfield from the R. Hilberg collection)

Rick Hilberg and his wife Carol seated at a table. They were accompanied by another woman who identified herself only as Suzanne.

Suzanne was a "contactee"—a person directly in touch with an alien intelligence. At least that was how she described herself. During a period of several hours, she related a long series of unusual—or extranormal—occurrences going back to her childhood. I won't go into detail, but suffice it to say that after lengthy discussion I was convinced Suzanne was telling the truth as she knew it. I was also convinced she was not a typical contactee—not merely passing along telepathic messages from "space brothers."

Rather, her experiences were much broader, much more involved. These included out-of-body phenomena, psychic phenomena, contact with noncorporeal (energy) entities, and brief, actual, clinical death. That Suzanne embodied (or hosted) a tremendous power, I have no doubt. During the course of our conversation she watched me carefully, and several times unnerved me with direct, piercing comments about my life, my past.

At one point she said, "You hold your pain close to you. You won't let it go." In that simple observation, prompted by nothing else in our dialogue, she touched all the agony, self-recrimination, and doubt I was embracing as a result of an emotionally wracking episode several years before. A few minutes later she disclosed her birthday—identical to my own: July 12.

This was nothing compared to what happened next. We were talking, surrounded by the sounds of the lounge—laughter, loud debate, pool balls clacking and falling. Without warning, Suzanne shifted to a kind of chant, or mantra. This penetrated the din, pulsing into my awareness.

I am not an easy subject for hypnosis. Professionals have found in me strong resistance to this state, and my efforts to employ auto-suggestive methods have had limited success, but within seconds I was slipping. I was locked to the cycle of her words, which she later described as a "now" affirmation. Abruptly, she broke the contact. Feeling dazed, I asked for an explanation. Suzanne laughed, offered a vague reply, and turned the conversation elsewhere. Then she did it again—a sledgehammer aimed at the psyche.

To say such an experience is unnerving is to greatly understate the issue. Still, I found myself enjoying Suzanne's company. When the lounge closed for the night, she decided to remain overnight rather than drive home. (She said she had not registered in advance for the conference, but attended spontaneously in order to try to meet other contactees or psychic channelers.) Unfortunately, the inn was already filled; no rooms were available. A LaQuinta Inn was located directly across the highway. I suggested she try the LaQuinta, and escorted her there. As she registered, an odd bit of synchronicity surfaced.

Several times during the evening Suzanne had used the expression "I grok"—a phrase (roughly equivalent to "I understand") coined by the late science-fiction writer Robert Heinlein in his novel *Stranger in a Strange Land.* I recall telling her that I had not heard that expression in many years. In the lobby of the LaQuinta, watching the desk clerk complete Suzanne's registration, I noticed a tired, worn paperback lying open on the lobby desk. The clerk was reading a copy of Heinlein's book.

* * *

After seeing Suzanne to her room, I returned to my own and immediately fell asleep. At breakfast Saturday morning I found myself seated with a young man I'll call John. He had traveled from the Midwest to the conference hoping to find help with contactee-type problems of his own. Again, I'll not go into detail. I will say, though, that John was greatly troubled. He appeared exhausted—as though he had not slept soundly in a week.

As I listened to his story, we were joined briefly by Gene Steinberg, and a short time later by Suzanne. I introduced her to John, hoping she might be able to help ease his state of mind. She listened as he again told his tale, and then quietly directed the conversation elsewhere. Later, I asked Suzanne why she failed to respond to John's story. She replied that any sharing of his experience would cause him to remain focused on his own unhappiness, thereby magnifying the problem. The only way to truly help, she said, was to direct his attention to something more positive and pleasant. This sounded plausible, so I let the subject drop, but it continued to nag at me.

Not until I was on the airplane, en route to Pennsylvania on the following day, did I finally recognize why Suzanne's response bothered me. I have been taught that if you can offer someone kindness, do it. If you can offer help, even if only in the most elementary way, then do so. To ignore, or fail to respond to, another's pain is simply to divorce oneself from the problem. Suzanne did not entirely ignore John's plea for help, but her effort to redirect his focus certainly left him believing that she did. Thinking about this on the airplane, I concluded that her way of helping was no help at all—only another way to avoid getting involved.

I met up with Suzanne again on Saturday afternoon, following a rather long presentation. Outside the lecture hall, we came upon Brad Steiger. I introduced the two only to discover that she and Brad were already acquainted.

Suzanne explained that she had been traveling one night when something "guided" her to a particular home in Scottsdale. When she rang the doorbell, Brad answered. Her verbal reaction at the time, she said, was something like: "I don't know who lives here or why I'm here, but I guess I'm supposed to be here." Brad, who was entertaining guests, invited Suzanne to join them.

Brad later admitted that the encounter pretty much happened the way Suzanne described it. When I told him about the disturbing power she demonstrated the previous night, he frowned thoughtfully and nodded. "Yes," he said, "there is a strange energy surrounding her."

Still later in the afternoon I was again in the lounge, involved in a conversation with Jim Vincent and Keith Michaels, editors of *Oddysey* (an intentional misspelling), a UFO research newsletter. Both men were young, and joined by Rick Hilberg we spanned a generation of UFO study.

I was acutely aware during that talk—as I think was Rick—of how much time had passed since he and I had first become involved in ufology. I discussed this with Gene Steinberg, who put it into words: "When we got involved, we learned from people like Moseley, Gray Barker, and [John] Keel," Gene said. "They were older, they had the experience. Now we're among the old-timers. Maybe it's our turn to be the teachers."

Maybe. But then maybe not.

My own view of the younger men and women at the conference—the newcomers to the field such as Vincent and Michaels—is that they were bright and capable. If there was any lack on their part, it was a tendency to disregard most views in ufology except

Hilberg and Allen H. Greenfield (at right) discussing the UFO phenomenon during a live radio show in Atlanta, Georgia in 1966. Greenfield would later emerge as one of the more original and provocative thinkers in ufology. (Photo by Don Cook from the R. Hilberg collection)

those focusing on the extraterrestrial hypothesis—the insistence that UFOs are alien spacecraft. This is a dogma that refuses to go away, and almost no one in the UFO community escapes its influence. Unfortunately, efforts to prove the ET hypothesis appear to be going nowhere—accounts of "crashed discs" and dead aliens notwithstanding.

There is, and has always been, reason to believe that the UFO phenomenon is representative of something far more complex than spacecraft and visiting extraterrestrials. This leads into areas of religion, philosophy, and metaphysics—the combination of which can leave a lasting, and disturbing, impression on the human psyche.

Frankly, I must admit that the ET hypothesis is a more attractive (or at least more easily understood) alternative. Furthermore, I am not saying that the ET concept is entirely wrong, only that it represents—for me, at least—too limited a view based on far too little information.

* * *

Saturday night was a banquet night, with Brad Steiger and his wife Sherry serving as guest speakers. I found myself at a table with the Hilbergs, Ed Biebel and his friend Mary from Tucson, and several others. As I looked around at the assembly, I noticed Suzanne seated off to one side with a number of women who all seemed to be paying her close attention. She must have sensed my gaze for she abruptly looked up and smiled. As the meal commenced, the conversation at my table escalated nicely, ranging from *Star Trek*, to Native American philosophy, to views on our troubled planetary environment. I was repeatedly surprised at the depth of concern evident whenever we touched on environmental issues, but I should not have been: whatever their personal or professional differences, the members of the UFO research community are nonetheless a fairly sensitive, issue-oriented group—far more so, I believe, than has ever been acknowledged by the popular media, or by the community itself. This view was upheld by the message in Sherry Steiger's softly delivered address—a message of hope, love, global awareness, and environmental concern.

Following the banquet, I walked outside and sat on the sidewalk in front of the lobby. The night air was warm, and I felt tremendously relaxed and at peace. As I sat there, a woman approached and asked if I knew of Suzanne's whereabouts. I recognized her as one of the women who had been seated with Suzanne. She admitted to having been captivated by the other's energy and charisma, and urgently wanted to speak with her again; but Suzanne was gone— vanished into the night without a word to her newfound friends.

About 1:00 A.M. Sunday, Moseley and Beckley assembled a group outside at the swimming pool, ostensibly to review the conference so that proposed future conventions might be better organized. At that point I realized something was absent, and had been missing from the conference all along: the bickering and strife I normally associated with such gatherings.

It was a welcome, refreshing absence.

Notes

1. In *Saucers and Saucerers* (Pan American New Physics Press, 1976, p. 48) Allen Greenfield observes that while the public forum at Moseley's 1967 New York convention attracted literally thousands of people, the "closed sessions"—the meetings not accessible to the general public—were so heavily attended that the number of participants for these sessions was actually greater than what one usually finds at entire UFO conventions.

2. Inner Light Publications, New Brunswick, New Jersey.

3. *Caveat Emptor* was first published by Gene Steinberg in autumn 1971, and ran fifteen issues before being discontinued. The magazine was resurrected in late 1988 for an eight-issue run—until the fall of 1990—before again being discontinued by Steinberg.

UFO Sighting
Summary 1947–1969

ON DECEMBER 17, 1969, the Secretary of the Air Force announced the termination of Project Blue Book, the Air Force program charged to investigate unidentified flying objects. Ostensibly intended as an impartial effort to evaluate the UFO phenomenon, Blue Book first operated as Project Grudge, a name taken from an earlier investigation (known also as Sign) that lasted from mid-1949 to mid-1950. The "new" Grudge was launched in 1951 and soon fell to the leadership of Captain Edward J. Ruppelt, an aeronautical engineer and World War II B-29 bombardier and radar operator. Not long after, the name of the project was changed to Blue Book.

Over the course of the years, Blue Book produced statistical data which has proven to be among the best available on the UFO subject. This was accomplished despite limited manpower and funding, and despite frequent internal and political opposition to the project.

Following the departure of Ruppelt in September 1953, the leadership of Blue Book fell to Capt. Charles A. Hardin for about two years, followed in turn by Capt. George Gregory, Lt. Col. Robert Friend, and Capt. Hector Quintanilla for varying periods of time. By the time the project ended, it was painfully evident that the more significant UFO reports were no longer going to Blue Book (if indeed they ever had been), but were being dispatched elsewhere within the Department of Defense.

What follows is a UFO sighting summary compiled by Blue Book. The summary reflects total reports received by the project from 1947 until 1969. In parentheses I have added the percentage of unidentified sightings for each year; these were not included in the original numbers.

When reading the summary, note how total sightings increased dramatically during the years 1952, 1957, 1965, 1966, and 1967. Note also how the percentage of unidentifieds rose steadily from 1948 until 1952, peaking at more than 20 percent of the reported sightings. In 1953 and 1954, the number of unidentifieds declined to something close to the pre-1952 level, after which the annual percentage tailed off dramatically, reaching less than 1 percent of reported sightings during the final two years of Blue Book.

The decline in the percentage of unidentifieds, from 1955 on, might be attributed to improved investigating techniques as well as an increased knowledge of the UFO phenomenon. It is more likely, however, that the declining numbers are attributable to a desire by Blue Book administrators to simply dismiss reports in the face of heightened official skepticism, and also due to the fact that—as noted—the better reports were already going elsewhere.

* * *

Year	Total Sightings	Unidentified
1947	122	12 (9.8%)
1948	156	7 (4.5%)
1949	186	22 (11.8%)
1950	210	27 (12.8%)
1951	169	22 (13%)
1952	1,501	303 (20.2%)
1953	509	42 (8.3%)
1954	487	46 (9.4%)
1955	545	24 (4.4%)
1956	670	14 (2.1%)
1957	1,006	14 (1.4%)
1958	627	10 (1.6%)
1959	390	12 (3.1%)
1960	557	14 (2.5%)
1961	591	13 (2.2%)
1962	474	15 (3.2%)
1963	399	14 (3.5%)
1964	562	19 (3.4%)
1965	887	16 (1.8%)
1966	1,112	32 (2.9%)
1967	937	19 (2%)
1968	375	3 (.8%)
1969	146	1 (.7%)

A Catalog of
Triangular UFO Reports

ON AUGUST 25, 1951, a high-level government worker and his wife watched in astonishment as a large, wedge-shaped object flew over their home in Albuquerque, New Mexico. The husband, an employee of the ultra-top-secret Sandia Corporation at Kirtland AFB, was in the backyard with his wife when the UFO passed silently overhead. The time was about 9:00 P.M.

In a report submitted to Project Blue Book, the couple said the UFO passed overhead at about 800 to 1,000 feet. They described it as "one and a half times the size of a B-36" with the wing "sharply swept back, almost like a V." On the trailing edge of the wing were "six to eight pairs of soft, glowing, bluish lights."[1] Twenty minutes later and some 300 miles to the east, four professors from Texas Technological College were sitting on a porch outside their home in Lubbock when a formation of "soft, glowing, bluish-green lights" flew overhead.[2] Two hours later they spotted a second set of lights. At about the same time, the wife of a retired Lubbock rancher was frightened while removing bed sheets from an outside clothesline by a large object that flew silently overhead. Rushing into the house, she located her husband and described the object as an "airplane without a body" trailing several pairs of glowing, bluish lights.[3]

Three hours after the initial sighting in Albuquerque, an Air Defense Command radar station in Washington State made contact with an object heading northwest at 13,000 feet at a speed of 900 miles per hour. The object was detected shortly after midnight, Pacific time, and tracked for six minutes on two separate scopes.[4] An F-86 jet fighter was scrambled to intercept, but the UFO was gone by the time the plane was aloft. Captain Edward Ruppelt, head of Project Blue Book, later calculated that if an aircraft had departed Lubbock at 11:20 P.M.—the time of the last known sighting near Lubbock that night—and flew nonstop to the radar station 1,300 miles away, it would have averaged 780 MPH—fairly close to the radar target's speed.

A check of Ruppelt's numbers show that his calculations were accurate: if the UFO flew at 780 MPH without changing course or speed, it would have passed within range of the station a few minutes after midnight, Pacific time. However, if the object had deviated from its path or paused en route for any significant time, its average speed would have been somewhat greater, say 900 MPH.

After a thorough investigation of the Albuquerque and Lubbock sightings, the Air Force failed to come up with an explanation that was both prosaic and acceptable to all involved. Numerous possibilities were listed, but only three were officially considered: (1) the glowing, bluish lights were atmospheric reflections from recently installed mercury-vapor street lamps; (2) they were streetlight reflections from groups of night-flying plovers (water birds the size of quail); (3) they were reflections from night-flying moths. None of the explanations took into account the fact that a large wedge- or wing-shaped body was seen in connection with the lights in at least two cases. Worse, the explanations belittled the testimony of the witnesses, of whom five were professionals in various fields of science. Finally, even the blue-suit investigators believed that the official explanations left much to be desired.

As for the August 26, 1951 radar sighting in Washington State, the Air Force officially concluded that it was caused by weather phenomena. They arrived at this conclusion even though the officer in charge of the radar facility—an Air Force captain—emphasized in his report that the UFO image was not a weather-related aberration. During an interview with Ruppelt, the station OIC was even more emphatic—commenting colorfully and heatedly about armchair investigators "miles from the closest radarscope."[5]

✭   ✭   ✭

The "Lubbock Lights," as they have come to be known, remain a tantalizing mystery after all these years. The caliber of the witnesses, the chronology of events, and the corresponding radar sighting all combine to set this series of events apart from the usual UFO scenario.

Adding to the unusual nature of the sightings are the descriptions of the object as a wedge-shaped wing or an "airplane without a body."

Accounts of wedge- or triangle-shaped UFOs were rare during the 1950s. They were an anomaly within a phenomenon heavily populated by flying spheres, cylinders, and aerial discs. In fact, reports of triangular UFOs only began to escalate around 1990, occurring at first gradually and then more sharply, until for a time the reports equaled (and quite possibly exceeded) those of classic disc-shaped UFOs.

In the following catalog, I have compiled a chronology of such reports. The catalog spans the decade of the nineties and has been drawn from various sources. This is not, by any stretch, a definitive list, although it does demonstrate the explosion of triangular-UFO sightings in the final decade of the twentieth century. A few of the reports, when correlated with additional information, suggest the presence and operation of prototype top-secret aircraft, and I have pointed this out wherever appropriate. I should also point out that the increase in these reports closely parallels the rise in popularity of the television series *The X-Files*, in which UFOs have been depicted as triangular craft. By the mid-1990s, the series had climbed from initial obscurity to acquire a strong, loyal audience in both the United States and the United Kingdom. Make of this what you will, but the influence of one on the other seems apparent.

Finally, I should state that the majority of reports in this catalog come from Great Britain (specifically England, Scotland, and Wales). This occurs not because Great Britain has more UFO activity than anywhere else, but because the citizens of the United Kingdom are not entirely blasé about the subject. As a result, UFO news coverage in the U.K. is substantial even if it is occasionally (and understandably) tongue-in-cheek.

★　★　★

Winter 1989–1990

Sightings of a triangular or delta-shaped flying object occurred in Belgium throughout the winter. The object was observed by both private citizens and military personnel, and also detected on military radar. In one widely publicized incident, two Belgium Air Force F-16 fighters were scrambled in pursuit. The UFO easily evaded the F-16s and broke their radar-lock by accelerating to speeds the fighters were unable to match. Tapes of the radar data were turned over to the Centre for the Study of Electronic Warfare. A photo of the UFO was computer enhanced, and determined to be of a delta-shaped object. (Numerous sources)

Summer/Fall 1990

A large, silent, triangular-shaped aircraft was observed on several occasions near Edwards AFB, California, and at other western U.S. locations, including Nevada, according to a report in *Aviation Week* and *Space Technology*. The magazine, citing "well qualified observers," said the aircraft had rounded wingtips and nose, and did not appear to have a vertical tail. One Nevada observer described the aircraft as "manta ray" shaped. Air Force officials had no comment on the reports.

February 1, 1993

A triangular UFO was spotted hovering over a water tank near Cedarburg, Wisconsin, at about 9:00 P.M. The object was dark with bright lights at the corners and a bank of white lights on one side. Police reported seeing beams of bright light coming from the vicinity of the water tank. (Charles Goldman, *Shepherd Express*, Milwaukee, Wisconsin, June 1993)

February 4, 1993

A beam of light from a "V-shaped" flying object reportedly hit a man in Beaver Dam, Wisconsin. The same day, at about 6:35 P.M., a triangular object was spotted near Star School Road and Highway 12, between Whiteside and Fort Atkinson. Witnesses said the object discharged a blue glowing ball that hung motionless in the sky. The triangular object moved with a blunt end forward and displayed a light at each point—one red and one blue light in front, and a white light at the back. A witness videotaped the UFO and the glowing ball. (Goldman)

September 26, 1993

Thirty witnesses observed a black triangular object as it flew over Bakewell, England. Time was about 9:30 P.M. The object had bright lights at the corners and red lights in between, and traveled at about forty miles per hour. The sighting was the first of many such reports in the county of Derbyshire. Between December 1994 and May 1995, a total of fifty-two sightings of triangular UFOs were documented in the area by investigators. (*Evening Telegraph*, Derby, England, September 28, 1993; also, Simon Burch, *Evening Telegraph*, October 8, 1996)

July 26, 1994

Numerous persons spotted a triangular object over Steelton, Pennsylvania, at about 11:00 P.M. The object—traveling at an estimated fifteen miles per hour—had a dark body or fuselage with lights underneath and white "headlights" in front. A spokesman for the UFO Contact Center in Federal Way, Washington, noted that it was unlikely the object was a secret prototype since it was brightly lit and flying in a heavily populated area. (Joseph J. Serwach, *Patriot News*, Harrisburg, Pennsylvania, July 28 and August 1, 1994)

October 10, 1994

Three witnesses—a woman and two men—watched a triangular object over Traverse City, Michigan, shortly after 8:00 P.M. The witnesses said the object had blue lights on the underside and a red light on top. As they stopped their vehicle for a better view, it rose into the sky and sped away. They said the angle of departure was similar to that of a helicopter, although the object made no sound. (*Record Eagle*, Traverse City, Michigan, November 1, 1998)

January 6, 1995

A British Airways Boeing 737 carrying sixty passengers was nearly hit by a wedge-shaped UFO while descending to Manchester Airport at 6:48 P.M. The aircraft was at 4,000 feet when the UFO passed it swiftly on the starboard (right) side. The pilot of the 737 said the object came so close that his co-pilot ducked. The crew reported that the object had small white lights, made no attempt to change course, made no sound, and created no turbulence as it passed by. An eyewitness on the ground also saw the object and described it as triangular. The UFO was not detected by airport radar. A year-long inquiry by the British Civil Aviation Authority failed to identify or trace the origin of the UFO. British authorities discounted suggestions that the object was a U.S. spy plane. (Various sources, most notably David Wallen, *Globe & Mail*, Toronto, Ontario, Canada, February 3, 1996)

February 13, 1995

An aircraft pilot residing in Westmoreland County, Pennsylvania, observed an unusual array of lights outside his home near Beaver Run Dam. The lights emanated from two huge triangular objects traveling "silently across the sky." (John M. Jennings, *The Dispatch*, Blairsville, Pennsylvania, February 9, 1996, from an original report by Stan Gordon)

July 23, 1995

Twelve passengers on a tour boat on Idaho's Snake River watched a "manta ray" shaped object pass overhead at about 11:00 P.M. The witnesses said the object ·was black and the wings appeared to "ripple." There was no report of lights on the object. Note: The manta ray shape and the appearance of wing ripple (see chapter 9), combined with a lack of aircraft lights and the remote location, suggest the test of a prototype aircraft equipped with an experimental camouflage. (Marianne Flagg, *The Idaho Statesman*, February 25, 1996)

September 24, 1995

A large, triangular-shaped "black mass" was seen hovering and moving slowly near Boise, Idaho. The object was observed at about 8:25 P.M. by at least two witnesses in different locations. Note: The absence of lights and relative proximity to the previous sighting suggest a prototype aircraft or stealth dirigible, although details are insufficient. (Flagg)

October 28, 1995

A yellow triangle-shaped UFO was spotted at about 2:30 A.M. by persons exiting a nightclub in Ilkeston, England, and by employees at a nearby parcel depot.

The glowing object was visible for about thirty minutes, hovering in the night sky. (*Advertiser*, Ilkeston, England, November 3, 1995)

November 4, 1995

A "pink triangle tipped with red lights" was spotted hovering above Pool in Cornwall, England. Eight witnesses observed the object. (*Sunday Independent*, Plymouth, England, December 17, 1995)

Late 1995–early 1996

Numerous triangular UFOs were reported in the vicinity of Lancaster and Morecambe, England. Witnesses described either a triangle with rounded edges or a proper triangle with a light at each corner. A newspaper reporter said the descriptions were similar to a triangular UFO shown on an episode of *The X-Files*. (Steve Jarvis, *Lancashire Evening Post*, Preston, England, January 17, 1996)

February 14, 1996

Crew members aboard two separate fishing boats spotted a triangular UFO during the evening hours, seventy miles southeast of Eyemouth, England. The exact time was not reported. The object was described as black with fifteen red lights along the side. The UFO was detected on each vessel's radarscope, after which the boats made radio contact to confer on the visual and radar observations. Crew members said the object moved slowly and was about "half the size of a football pitch." Two jet fighters reportedly overflew the area fifteen minutes after the UFO had departed. The Ministry of Defence denied the presence of military aircraft. The British UFO Research Association (BUFORA) investigated the incident. (Sandy Brydon, *Berwickshire News*, England, October 3, 1996)

March 1, 1996

Motorists reported a triangular flying object near Meols Cop Road in Southport, England, at about 6:00 P.M. One witness said the object had a white light at each corner and a square green light in the middle. He said it moved around over a field, then stopped and transformed into a single large green light that flew away. (*Visitor*, Southport, England, March 8, 1996)

March 9, 1996

At about 10:50 P.M., five people at Gallows Corner in Romford, England, watched a large triangular-shaped object with white lights at each corner and a pulsating orange light in the center. Similar reports were widespread throughout the area. (Dan Humphreys, *Romford Recorder*, Essex, England, March 15, 1996)

May 3, 1996

A postal employee reported seeing a "massive" triangular object over Winshill, England, during a period of high UFO activity in the region. (*Burton Mail*, Staffordshire, England, May 21, 1996)

May 4, 1996

Two teenage boys fishing near Milverton, England, reported the appearance of a large, black triangle in the sky. The object displayed a light in the center and a white light at each corner, and made a low-pitched humming sound. The incident occurred at about 8:30 P.M. (*Sunday Independent*, Plymouth, England, May 5, 1996)

June 17, 1996

A large, black triangular object was spotted at about 10:30 P.M. by a Pensacola, Florida, motorist en route home from work. The motorist, a young man, was eastbound on Kingsfield Road north of Pensacola when the object drew near. He pulled his vehicle to the side of the road, as did a motorist towing a boat trailer ahead of him. The object had a single white light at each corner and hovered directly over the road. A red blinking light was at the center of the triangle. The object remained over the road for about twenty seconds before moving away—slowly at first and then more rapidly—until it was gone from view. (Carole Baker, "Triangular Shaped Craft Hovers Over Witness," *Islander,* Pensacola Beach, Florida, July 10, 1996)

July 17, 1996

A Damiansville, Illinois, woman reported a triangular flying object near Interstate 64, southeast of Damiansville, at about 9:00 A.M. The witness was in a vehicle approaching an interstate ramp when she saw the object, which appeared to be shiny, like "polished steel." The UFO hovered in one location over trees for four or five minutes before vanishing. The witness said there was no sound or contrail from the object. (*The Times,* Okawville, Illinois, July 31, 1996)

September 15, 1996

A Glenrothes, Scotland, man spotted a "perfectly equilateral triangle," gray in color, while attempting to get a look at the planet Jupiter with binoculars. The witness said he was glassing the sky at about 9:00 P.M. when the object moved across his field of vision, traveling from west to east in a straight line. The sighting lasted about ten seconds. He said the object displayed no position lights, and the only reason he saw it was because of a clear sky and bright moonlight. Note: The precise shape, the level trajectory, the color, and absence of lights all suggest a prototype aircraft and not a classic UFO. (*Evening Telegraph,* Dundee, Scotland, September 17, 1996)

January 5, 1997

The *London Sunday Mirror* published a photo of a silver triangle flying over the Lancashire moors. The cameraman, identified only as a landscape photographer, was shooting snow scenes on the moors (time and date not reported, though the incident was evidently recent) when he noticed "a slight movement" through the viewfinder. When he looked up, the distraction was gone. Later, when he developed the film, he discovered the image of a small silver triangle in the center of a photo frame. Commenting on the photo, the *Mirror* referred to the respected *Jane's Military Aircraft* and a British stealth project known as HALO (High Altitude, Low Observable). A Ministry of Defence spokesman denied any knowledge of HALO. Denials aside, this one was probably a prototype aircraft. (Alan Rimmer, *Sunday Mirror*, London, January 5, 1997)

February 14, 1997

A bicyclist riding along the bank of Roman Lakes at Marple Bridge, England, reported a late evening encounter with a large, gray triangular object hovering above the water. The report was telephoned to a research group known as Quest International. A spokesman for Quest said he doubted the report was a hoax, noting that the caller sounded "really frightened." (Richard Partington, *Stockport Express Advertiser*, Cheshire, England, February 26, 1997)

February 25, 1997

A triangle-shaped UFO reportedly hovered over a car occupied by a teenaged driver and an eleven-year-old passenger as the two drove home to Oswestry from Shrewsbury in Salop County, England. The incident occurred on the Shrewsbury to Four Crosses road. The time of the incident was not reported. The driver said the UFO hovered, shot out a flame, and then vanished. An RAF spokesman said that it was unlikely the object was a military aircraft on a night training flight. (*Shropshire Star*, Wellington, England, March 10, 1997)

Summer 1997

A dark triangular flying object was frequently observed in the vicinity of Lancaster, England, during a period that lasted several months. The object was described as at least twice the size of a 747 jumbo jet, and witnesses said it sometimes emitted blinding flashes of white light from each corner. (Fiona May, *People*, London, England, August 17, 1997)

June 1997

A black triangle-shaped object, illuminated by a full moon, was observed flying over Lake Laberge in the Canadian Yukon. The object made a "loud noise" but displayed no lights and left no contrail. The exact date and time of the incident are unknown. Note: The isolated area, sound, and lack of lights suggest a prototype aircraft. (Jim Bronskill, *National Post*, Toronto, Canada, December 22, 1998, from a UFO batch report released by the Canada Defense Department)

September 9, 1997

A Yorkshire man reported seeing a black, triangle-shaped object over Wakefield, England, at about 11:30 P.M. The witness, an active UFO investigator, said similar reports had come from various locations in the area. He said the object was dark with red lights on the underside and made no sound. (*Evening Post*, Yorkshire, England, September 12, 1997)

October 8, 1997

A Hillsboro, Ohio, resident reported seeing a triangle-shaped flying object surrounded by jet aircraft—as many as thirteen jets, the witness said. The UFO "rose straight up" and vanished from view. The time was not reported. (Joseph Trainor, *UFO Roundup*, October 19, 1997)

October 11-12, 1997

Three teenage girls reported a disc-like UFO and a triangular object flying together near Burnley, England, on the night of October 11. The same night, a man at a different location also reported a triangular UFO. A bright sphere of light was spotted the following night above Trawden. (Tim Nixon, *Citizen*, Burnley, England, October 16, 1997)

October 14, 1997

Four separate sightings of a large, black triangular UFO were reported in Somerset, England. (*Western Daily Press*, Bristol, England, October 21, 1997)

November 1997

A triangular UFO with bright white lights at each corner was observed over Manston, England. Witnesses said the object was moving faster than any jet aircraft and made a high-pitched "screaming sound." Exact date and time were not reported. (*Thanet Times*, Kent, England, November 18, 1997)

November 21, 1997

The occupants of a car traveling along A1307, en route to Four Wentways, Abington, England, reported a slow-moving, triangular flying object at about 9:30 P.M. The occupants, a husband and wife, said the UFO had a green light on one corner and a red light on another, with a white light underneath. The object was silent and moved at about twenty MPH. (*Evening News*, Cambridge, England, November 24, 1997)

December 8, 1997

A large, black triangular flying object was reported over central Walthamstow, England, at about 11:37 P.M. Witnesses said the object appeared to be flying at about

10,000 to 15,000 feet. No other details were reported. (*Yellow Advertiser,* Colchester, England, January 9, 1998)

January 24, 1998

A Swansea, Wales, motorist encountered a black triangular flying object as she traveled west on M4 toward Severn Bridge at about 3:15 P.M. The witness said the object passed within 300 yards of her vehicle. (*South Wales Evening Post,* Swansea, Wales, January 29, 1998)

March 1998

A black triangular object was reported hovering above Hartlebury Common, near Stourport, England. UFO sightings were numerous in the area. (*Express & Stars,* Wolverhampton, England, March 14, 1998)

March 3, 1998

A brightly lit, triangular UFO was spotted over Mansfield, England, at about 11:50 P.M. The object hovered for ten minutes before darting away to the southeast. The British UFO Association investigated the report. (*Mansfield & Sutton Observer,* Mansfield, England, March 12, 1998)

March 18, 1998

A woman looking out a house window in Vancouver, British Columbia, spotted a triangular formation of bright white lights. The sighting occurred at night, but the time was not reported. The witness said the object paused before racing away to the west. Reports of triangular UFOs were numerous in the area at the time. (*Province,* Vancouver, British Columbia, Canada, March 25, 1998)

March 27-30, 1998

Numerous reports of triangular UFOs were reported in Stafford, England. Some of the objects displayed white lights, others red, white, and blue lights. (Jenny Amphlett, *Post*, Stafford, England, April 9, 1998)

April 1998

Five witnesses, including a vicar, spotted a triangular UFO hovering over Maiden Castle in Dorchester, England. The castle dates to the Iron Age. Time and date of the sighting were not given, though details suggest the incident occurred on April 14 or 15. Witnesses said the object was a triangle when first observed, but changed into a sphere before it flew off. (*Dorset Evening Echo*, Weymouth, England, April 15, 1998)

April 10, 1998

Two high-school students in Pueblo, Colorado, reported seeing a triangular object in the southwest sky at 9:07 P.M. The two boys, each seventeen, said the object zigzagged in flight and appeared to scan the area with a spotlight. They said the UFO circled a southbound passenger jet and changed shape, dividing into different colors. "It looked like cells dividing," one of the witnesses said. The boys said the jet departed at high speed after being circled by the UFO. (Peter Strescino, *Pueblo Chieftain*, April 19, 1998)

May 27, 1998

Twin brothers in East Kilbride, Scotland, reported seeing a triangular object over their home at about 12:30 A.M. The object was silent and displayed a bright white light at the front. UFO sightings, including reports of classic discs, were numerous in the area at the time. (Susie Kelly, *East Kilbride News*, Lanarkshire, England, May 27, 1998)

June 3, 1998

Two individuals traveling the road between Llanidloes and Newtown, Wales, reported seeing three hovering "perfect triangles." The UFOs remained motionless for several minutes before they began a slow movement and then darted away. The incident occurred at about 10:30 P.M. An RAF spokesman suggested that the sighting might have been an illusion caused by aircraft lighting or a laser light show. (*County Times*, Welshpool, Wales, June 12, 1998)

June 26, 1998

Two individuals spotted a triangular UFO hovering above Corbett Hospital in Stourbridge, England. The sighting occurred during the early morning hours. The witnesses said the UFO had four white lights at each corner and projected a white beam onto buildings. (*Express & Star*, Wolverhampton, England, July 10, 1998)

August 14, 1998

A retired husband and his wife spotted a UFO which, at first, appeared triangular but later, from a different angle, appeared oval. The UFO was reported above Hastings, England, at about 9:00 P.M. The object displayed lights that changed color and pattern depending on the angle of view. (*Observer*, Hastings, England, August 21, 1998)

September 21, 1998

A slow-moving, V-shaped UFO displaying red-and-white rapidly flashing lights was observed by several individuals as it passed overhead, traveling from the area of Nantwich to Crewe, England. Police were notified and at least one officer subsequently spotted the object. The incident occurred at about 2:00 A.M. Air traffic controllers at the Manchester airport said they detected nothing on radar. (*Crewe Chronicle*, Cheshire, England, September 23, 1998)

October 15, 1998

A gray triangular object was reported hovering near Georgia's Kennesaw Mountain at about 12:30 P.M. The witness said the object flew north, then changed shape to a disc before vanishing. (Letter published in the *Journal & Constitution*, Atlanta, Georgia, November 8, 1998)

October 16, 1998

A woman reported a diamond-shaped UFO over Corstorphine Hill, Edinburgh, Scotland, at about 11:30 P.M. The object displayed red and white lights. (*Evening News*, Edinburgh, Scotland, October 23, 1998)

October 18, 1998

Three Wombourne, England, residents observed a strange, motionless sphere in the sky at Sandwell Valley at about 12:40 P.M. The sphere was in view for about twenty minutes when a metallic-looking triangular UFO also appeared. The witnesses said the triangle moved from side to side "in short bursts" before vanishing completely. The sphere remained in its original location but dwindled to a dark spot. The overall sighting lasted about thirty minutes. (*Express & Star*, Wolverhampton, England, October 29, 1998; also the *Wolverhampton Chronicle*, January 22, 1999)

January 10, 1999

A husband and wife traveling by auto between Burley Woodhead and Ilkley, England, spotted a dart-like UFO. The witnesses said the object was illuminated on the underside by two rows of lights, and that the lights were so bright they obscured the finer details of the object. The sighting occurred in the afternoon, though no time was stated. The witnesses noted that commercial aircraft were visible at the time, but the UFO looked nothing like them. (*Ilkley Gazette*, Yorkshire, England, January 14, 1999)

January 21, 1999

A large, shiny triangular UFO was sighted around 4:00 P.M. in the vicinity of Southport, England. Several witnesses observed the object. (Sam Thomas, *Champion*, Southport, England, February 3, 1999)

February 1999

A student driver and her instructor were surprised by the sight of a "triangle shaped object" hovering over Hermitage Road in Upper Norwood, England. The incident occurred around dusk, though the date and exact time were not reported. According to the driving instructor, other individuals also observed the object. Police dismissed the sighting as an airship scheduled to pass through the area that same evening. (*Guardian*, Croydon, England, February 17, 1999)

March 10, 1999

A motorist traveling through Duffield, England, spotted a bright light in the sky at about 11:00 P.M., and pulled into a bus stop for a better view. As the object flew overhead, the motorist said she could clearly see a "flat, triangular, black shape with equal sides, flying point first." On the same night, at about 10:45 P.M., a resident of Belper, England, observed a "flying triangle" while letting her cat into the garden. The witness said she initially saw a bright orange light, but after retrieving a pair of binoculars observed that the orange light appeared to be at the front of a "perfect, black triangle." A row of red lights illuminated one side of the triangle, which was flying slowly and silently just over the roof tops, the witness said. The object vanished from view behind neighboring houses. (Phil Stubbs, *Evening Telegraph*, Derby, England, March 31, 1999)

March 23, 1999

An object shaped like "a black wedge of cheese" was spotted during the night by at least five people as it passed over Brinsley, Crich, and Belper, England. Some witnesses said it flew slowly, with a blunt end forward, and had two white "headlamps" along the leading edge. Another individual said the object changed shape, from a diamond to a triangle, while yet another reported seeing only a flying triangle. (*Belper News*, Derbyshire, England, March 24, 1999)

April 4, 1999

An object displaying three orange lights in a triangular formation was spotted over Poole, England, at about 10:00 P.M. A former British gas line worker, his wife, and two friends from the vicinity of Mill Lane, Parkstone, observed the object. The sighting continued for three to four minutes and was identical to an occurrence on March 18 at 10:45 P.M., at the same location. The witness in the earlier case was a retired Merchant Navy officer who said the lights moved slowly at about twenty MPH. (*Advertiser*, Poole, England, April 8, 1999)

May 7–9, 1999

A White Rock, British Columbia, man observed a giant "blue plasma ball" cruising over Semiahmoo Bay shortly before 10:00 P.M. on May 7. The following night, again at about 10:00 P.M., three White Rock residents spotted a huge boomerang-shaped object. The UFO was illuminated along the leading edge by eight lights. The witnesses—two women and an eleven-year-old girl—were at a McDonald's restaurant on Johnston Road when they saw the UFO. They said it moved slowly for about eight seconds before disappearing from view. Five minutes later, two women on the pier at White Rock spotted a wedge or triangle-shaped UFO, which they observed for several minutes as it moved across Semiahmoo Bay. On May 9, at about 10:30 P.M., a man and woman spotted a wedge-shaped flying object over Highway 99 near Crescent Road. The witnesses said the object had flashing red and blue lights. They also reported seeing a flare-like amber flash, possibly originating from a second object. (Tom Zytaruk, *Now*, Surrey, British Columbia, May 15, 1999)

October 9, 1999

Two men fishing in Pensacola Pass, near Pensacola Beach, Florida, spotted an object that appeared triangular in shape. The witnesses, a former Air Force security policeman and a retired Army helicopter pilot (employed as a police officer), said the UFO traveled west over the Gulf of Mexico, moving silently in an erratic zigzag manner. The object changed locations quickly and hovered at least four times. An intense blue arcing—akin to discharge electricity—surrounded the object. Three lights were visible on the object in a triangular formation, glowing variably blue to pale yellow. An FM radio in the possession of the anglers was disrupted by static. A trailing helicopter sound was said to have been heard when the UFO first appeared, but no helicopter was seen. An aircraft departing nearby Sherman Field turned away from the UFO—the pilot seemingly unaware of anything unusual in the vicinity. At one point the object hovered for about a minute and a half over the southwestern boundary of Pensacola Naval Air Station. One of the two witnesses experienced nausea as a result of the incident, the nausea lasting about ten minutes. The object was under observation from about 7:57 P.M. until 8:12 P.M. (*Islander*, Gulf Breeze, Florida, November 17, 1999, from a report provided by Peter Davenport of the National UFO Reporting Center in Seattle)

November 6, 1999

Three individuals in Matawan, New Jersey, reported seeing a large, triangle-shaped object pass overhead as they were settling into a Jacuzzi. The object was illuminated by pale orange lights and moved southwest at what was described as an extremely slow speed. The sighting occurred at about 6:03 P.M. (George Filer, *MUFON UFO Journal*, from a report provided by Peter Davenport of the National UFO Reporting Center)

November 16, 1999

A Middletown, Ohio, resident reported seeing a huge triangular object made up of pulsating green lights. The sighting occurred at about 9:00 P.M. and lasted about ten seconds. The witness, who was in front of a neighbor's house, said the object passed silently overhead. A police dispatcher contacted by the witness said the object was probably part of the Leonid meteor shower—a conclusion the witness disagreed with, noting that the object appeared to be a machine of some kind. An unusual number of aircraft were observed in the area following the sighting. (National UFO Reporting Center and the *Ohio UFO Notebook #21*, 2000)

November 18, 1999

An individual about one mile west of Ohio State University spotted a dark flying object in the shape of an equilateral triangle around 1:00 A.M. At about 1:50 A.M., a suburban Columbus, Ohio, police officer and a reserve officer for a different department riding with the first officer spotted the same object or one virtually identical to it. The object was visible for five to fifteen seconds and was initially observed moving east to west. The officers, who exited their cruiser car for a better view, said the UFO was silent and made a slow banking turn to the right. As it did so a dark underside was revealed, devoid of lights but distorted as if somehow camouflaged. The object—close enough to the witnesses so that sharp, defined edges could be seen despite the distortion and lack of illumination—completed a ninety-degree turn to the north while banking and then leveled off. The suburban Columbus officer said the object seemed to glide through the air much as a stingray glides through the water. The object was described as large—much larger than a police helicopter—and also moved more slowly than the average speed of a helicopter. A check by the officer with personnel at Port Columbus Airport revealed that nothing unusual had been detected on radar. Note: The lack of lights and the presence of an apparent distortion field, along with the clearly defined triangular outline (many UFOs are described as having a hazy or somewhat indistinct form), suggest a prototype aircraft. (National UFO Reporting Center and the *Ohio UFO Notebook #21*, 2000)

December 12, 1999

A bright light traveling from the northwest—initially believed to be the landing lights of an aircraft from West Chester County airport—drew the rapt attention of a Pleasantville, New York, man when it abruptly halted in midair. The witness, who was in his living room watching from a window, observed a second light appear after about twenty seconds and then both lights began to move slowly west. The witness retrieved a pair of binoculars and was able to focus on one of the lights, which under magnification appeared to be three separate white lights forming the corners of an equilateral triangle. A red light—more faint than the white lights—was at the center of the triangle. The sighting occurred at about 10:09 P.M., and the triangular object remained in view about three minutes. (Joseph Trainor, *UFO Roundup*, Vol. 4, No. 34)

January 2, 2000

A large V-shaped UFO was spotted in the vicinity of Endeavor Hills, Victoria, Australia, by a resident feeding his dogs. The time was about 10:50 P.M. The object, which blocked out the Big Dipper constellation, was described as a V-shape, solid black in color, and about five times the size of a jumbo jet. Dim orange lights were observed along the front of the object, which made no sound. The object remained in view for about four seconds. (Alice Mitchell, AUFORN, and Keith Basterfield, Network Australia)

January 5, 2000

A Highland, Illinois, resident and part-time truck driver was returning home after delivering dry goods in Bloomington, when he spotted a huge, lighted object in the night sky. The time was around 4:00 A.M. The driver had just stopped to check on his other business—a miniature golf course on the north side of Highland—when the object slowly approached from the northeast. He described it as being as large as a

football field with red and white lights, and said it was
no more than 500 to 700 feet off the ground. He
reported the object to Highland police, and a call was
made to a radio dispatcher in St. Clair County.

As a result of the call to St. Clair County, police in
Lebanon, Illinois were notified, and a few minutes
later—at about 4:11 A.M.—a patrolling officer radioed
that he had spotted "a very bright light just east of
town," approximately six miles from his location. The
officer gave chase and caught up with the UFO near the
village of Summerfield. Parking his cruiser, the officer
shut off both the overhead lights and the engine and
waited as the object passed slowly overhead at an altitude of about 1,000 to 1,500 feet. The officer later
reported that the UFO made absolutely no sound.

Police officers in the communities of Shiloh (about
seven miles from Lebanon), Millstadt, and Dupo also
subsequently spotted the object. All described it as
"arrowhead" shaped or like an elongated, narrow triangle, and all said it was huge and unlike any known type
of aircraft. The object was under observation by the
various officers for approximately an hour as it traveled
along a northeast to southwest flight path that covered
about sixty miles.

Some two hours later, at about 6:45 A.M., the object
was again spotted, this time west of the Interstate 225
overpass, in the vicinity of the Frank Holton State Park.
The witness was a 50-year-old English teacher en route
to his job at East St. Louis High School. He said he
spotted the object as the sun came up, and described it
as large, illuminated, and arrowhead shaped. There was
no explanation for where the object had been during
the two hours between the police sightings and the
observation made by the English teacher. (Valerie
Schremp, *Post Dispatch*, St. Louis, Missouri, January 9,
2000; also Sherry Kirk, *The Progress*, O'Fallon, Illinois,
January 13, 2000, and the *Riverfront Times*, St. Louis,
Missouri, April 5, 2000)

Notes

1. Edward J. Ruppelt, *The Report on Unidentified Flying Objects* (New York, Doubleday & Company, Inc., 1956), pp. 96, 97.

2. Ibid., p. 97.

3. Ibid., p. 104.

4. Ibid., pp. 97, 98.

5. Ibid., p. 109.

The KYW Photograph

On a Thursday night in September 1963, Allan J. Manak and Earl J. Neff were taking a turn as guest speakers for a program called "Ufology Roundtable," a weekly two-hour broadcast on KYW Radio in Cleveland. During the broadcast, the show's host, Harv Morgan, presented Manak with a photograph and asked for an opinion.

"Needless to say, the photograph had me flabbergasted," Manak later related.[1]

Mailed anonymously to the radio station in an envelope postmarked Orrville, Ohio (a town about forty miles south of Cleveland), the black-and-white photo showed a classic disc, complete with dome, positioned at a slight angle over a cornfield. The bottom of the object was in dark shadow and the upper left glistened in apparent sunlight.

The following week, Manak was back on the air and informed Morgan's listeners that he had had the photo enlarged by two professional photographers, Donald Brill and George Shuba, who at

213

the time operated a studio in downtown Cleveland.[2] He said the photographers had enlisted the aid of two other individuals—one an expert in the field of optics, the other an experienced photo analyst—and supplied them with five enlargements of assorted size and contrast. After a thorough study, the opinion rendered by the experts was that the photo did not appear to be a hoax.

Said Manak: "Analysis indicated that the photo was taken at about either 8:00 A.M. or 4:00 P.M. The object seemed to be metallic and approximately thirty to forty feet in diameter, and located an estimated 2,500 feet from the camera. Obviously, these estimates ruled out the possibility that [the UFO] could have been a model or some type of toy."[3]

A different opinion was rendered by members of the Cleveland Ufology Project, then chaired by Neff. The project had submitted a copy of the photo to members of a UFO research group in Akron, Ohio, and the Akron group had concluded that the photo was doctored because of suspicious scratch marks surrounding the UFO image and because of a stain on the photo. But according to Manak, the photo studied by the Akron group was a third generation copy made from a second generation print that he had given to Neff from the original in his possession. The original print, Manak said, had no stain and no scratch marks.[4]

Manak, who died in November 1999, believed that the object in the photo was most likely what it appeared to be—a genuine UFO. However, any certainty about the "KYW photograph," as it has come to be known, lies with the anonymous individual (the photographer, presumably) who mailed it from Orrville, Ohio. That individual remains unknown and undeclared to this day.

Allan J. Manak believed that the object in the photo sent to Cleveland radio station KYW in 1963 was most likely what it appeared to be—a genuine UFO. "The object seemed to be metallic and approximately thirty to forty feet in diameter, and located an estimated 2,500 feet from the camera."

Notes

1. Allan Manak's account about the "KYW photograph" appeared in *Northern Ohio UFO Casebook*, compiled by Rick R. Hilberg (self-published, March 1997), p. 6.

2. The studio was Commerce Photo, located at 238 The Arcade, Cleveland.

3. Manak, *Northern Ohio UFO Casebook*, p. 6.

4. Ibid, p.7.

* * *

To report a UFO sighting or event, contact:

National UFO Reporting Center
P.O. Box 45623
University Station
Seattle, WA 98145
Telephone hotline: 206-722-3000
Web site: www.ufocenter.com

Mutual UFO Network (MUFON)
P.O. Box 369
Morrison, Colorado 80465-0369
Telephone hotline: 1-800-836-2166
Web site: www.mufon.org

* * *

SUGGESTED READING

FOR THOSE INTERESTED in further reading, the following book list may be of interest. Some of these books are no longer in print, although used copies are frequently available at secondhand stores and from vendors at UFO and science-fiction conventions.

UFO Crash Landing: The Full Story of the Rendlesham Forest Close Encounter. Jenny Randles—Blandford (UK), 1998 (trade edition).

Night Siege: The Hudson Valley UFO Sightings. Dr. J. Allen Hynek, Philip J. Imbrogno, and Bob Pratt—Llewellyn, 1998 (trade).

Angels and Aliens: UFOs and the Mythic Imagination. Keith Thompson—Fawcett Columbine, 1991 (trade).

Operation Trojan Horse. John A. Keel—Putnam, 1970 (hardcover); IllumiNet Press, 1991 (trade).

The Mothman Prophecies. John A. Keel—Saturday Review Press, 1975 (hardcover); Signet, 1976 (paperback); IllumiNet Press, 1991 (trade).

Unexplained. Jerome Clark—Visible Ink Press, 1993 (trade).

Passport to Magonia. Jacques Vallee—Contemporary Books, 1993 (trade).

The Report on Unidentified Flying Objects. Edward J. Ruppelt—Doubleday, 1956 (hardcover).

The Mysterious Valley. Christopher O'Brien—St. Martin's Press, 1996 (paperback).

INDEX

☾ REACH FOR THE MOON

Llewellyn publishes hundreds of books on your favorite subjects! To get these exciting books, including the ones on the following pages, check your local bookstore or order them directly from Llewellyn.

Order by Phone
- Call toll-free within the U.S. and Canada, 1-800-THE MOON
- In Minnesota, call (651) 291-1970
- We accept VISA, MasterCard, and American Express

Order by Mail
- Send the full price of your order (MN residents add 7% sales tax) in U.S. funds, plus postage & handling to:
  Llewellyn Worldwide
  P.O. Box 64383, Dept. 0-7387-0106-8
  St. Paul, MN 55164–0383, U.S.A.

Postage & Handling
- **Standard** (U.S., Mexico, & Canada)
If your order is:
  $20.00 or under, add $5.00
  $20.01–$100.00, add $6.00
  Over $100, shipping is free
(Continental U.S. orders ship UPS. AK, HI, PR, & P.O. Boxes ship USPS 1st class. Mex. & Can. ship PMB.)
- **Second Day Air** (Continental U.S. only): $10.00 for one book + $1.00 per each additional book
- **Express** (AK, HI, & PR only) [Not available for P.O. Box delivery. For street address delivery only.]: $15.00 for one book + $1.00 per each additional book
- **International Surface Mail:** Add $1.00 per item
- **International Airmail:** Books—Add the retail price of each item; Non-book items—Add $5.00 per item

Please allow 4–6 weeks for delivery on all orders.
Postage and handling rates subject to change.

Discounts
We offer a 20% discount to group leaders or agents. You must order a minimum of 5 copies of the same book to get our special quantity price.

Free Catalog

Get a free copy of our color catalog, *New Worlds of Mind and Spirit*. Subscribe for just $10.00 in the United States and Canada ($30.00 overseas, airmail).

Visit our website at www.llewellyn.com for more information.

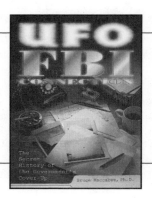

UFOs Over Topanga Canyon
Eyewitness Accounts
of the California Sightings

Preston Dennett

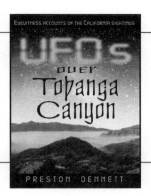

The rural Californian community of Topanga Canyon is home to 8,000 close-knit residents, the Topanga State Park—and an unusual amount of strange activity going on in the sky.

Like Hudson Valley, N.Y., and Gulf Breeze, Fla., Topanga Canyon is considered a UFO hotspot, with sightings that began more than fifty years ago and continue to this day. Here is the first book to present the activity in the witnesses' own words.

Read new cases of unexplained lights, metallic ships, beams of light, face-to-face alien encounters, UFO healings, strange animal sightings, animal mutilations, and evidence of a government cover-up. There are even six cases involving missing time abductions, and a possible onboard UFO experience.

1-56718-221-6, 312 pp., 5 3/16 x 8, illus.   **$12.95**

Extraterrestrial Visitations
True Accounts of Contact

Preston Dennett

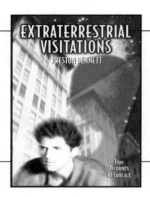

This book represents the cutting edge of UFO abduction research, with ten new and original firsthand accounts of very close contact with UFOs and aliens. Told in the witnesses' own words, the stories have immediacy, objectivity, and credibility. What's more, the majority of cases come from fully conscious experiences, as opposed to cases that rely on memories retrieved through hypnosis.

Several of the stories present new information that is highly controversial and not commonly reported in the UFO literature, including healings, the presence of the military during an abduction, channeled information, reports of underground bases, premonitions of future disaster, praying mantis-type aliens, benevolent encounters, and much more.

1-56718-220-8, 288 pp., 5 3/16 x 8   **$12.95**

To order call 1-800-THE MOON
Prices subject to change without notice

Contact of the 5th Kind
The silent invasion has begun

Philip J. Imbrogno &
Marianne Horrigan

George and Maria have a daughter who is almost two years old. One day she brought out her doll and asked her mom to open its head. Maria asked her where she had seen something like that and she told her mom, "They do it to daddy at night."

How would the people of this country react if they knew that their government allowed an alien intelligence to abduct them and experiment on them in exchange for technological advances?

Contact of the 5th Kind is a new approach to UFO research that is filled with hundreds of documented alien contact and abduction cases. Philip J. Imbrogno is one of the few researchers who actually goes out into the field to personally investigate the evidence. And the evidence, in some cases, is so overwhelming that even the most skeptical of readers will not be able to deny that there is an intelligence currently interacting with certain people on this planet.

1-56718-361-1, 256 pp., 5 3/16 x 8   **$9.95**

To order call 1-800-THE MOON
Prices subject to change without notice

True Hauntings
Spirits with a Purpose

Hazel M. Denning, Ph.D.

Do spirits feel and think? Does death automatically promote them to a paradise—or as some believe, a hell? Real-life ghost-buster Dr. Hazel M. Denning reveals the answers through case histories of the friendly and hostile earthbound spirits she has encountered. Learn the reasons spirits remain entrapped in the vibrational force field of the earth: fear of going to the other side, desire to protect surviving loved ones, and revenge. Dr. Denning also shares fascinating case histories involving spirit possession, psychic attack, mediumship, and spirit guides. Find out why spirits haunt us in *True Hauntings*, the only book of its kind written from the perspective of the spirits themselves.

1-56718-218-6, 240 pp., 6 x 9   **$12.95**

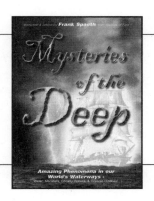

Mysteries of the Deep
Amazing Phenomena
in our World's Waterways

Edited by Frank Spaeth

I snapped a look out the window. The right wing had simply disappeared from sight! It was an eerie feeling, as though we'd flown into some impossible limbo. I then noticed that what had been blue sky had changed to a creamy yellow, as though we were in the middle of a bottle of eggnog.
   —"The Triangle with Four (or More) Sides"

Thinking of going deep sea fishing? You'll think again after you read *Mysteries of the Deep*, a compilation of the best sea stories from the past 47 years of FATE magazine. From Atlantis to the Bermuda Triangle, from the Loch Ness Monster to giant jellyfish, you'll find more than a few reasons to stay out of the water. The reports presented here come from the personal experiences of the average citizen as well as the detailed investigations of well-known authors such as Martin Caidin, Dr. Karl P. N. Shuker, Jerome Clark, and Mark Chorvinsky.

1-56718-260-7, 256 pp., 5 3/16 x 8, illus.   **$9.95**

To order call 1-800-THE MOON
Prices subject to change without notice

Out of Time and Place
Amazing Accounts that Challenge
Our View of Human History

Edited by Terry O'Neill

*I held my hand out of the wagon window and caught four fat,
brown little toads . . . I had heard of fish and frogs falling from the
clouds, but I had never heard of a fall of toads . . .*
— "Does it Rain Toads?"

Explore fascinating mysteries of history, archaeology, and the
paranormal with this collection of amazing reports published only
in the pages of FATE magazine. The writers of these fascinating
articles follow the footsteps of Indiana Jones, seeking the lost and
trying to solve the mysteries of the oddly found. Thirty original
articles from the best of FATE over the past forty years feature
tales of lost cities, strange falls from the sky, extraordinary creatures, and misplaced artifacts that call into question our entire
view of human history.

Despite studies by historians and scientists from many fields,
these events and objects from out of time and place remain unexplained. Readers can't resist being enthralled by these mysteries
and by the efforts to solve them.

1-56718-261-5, 272 pp., 5 3/16 x 8   **$9.95**

To order call 1-800-THE MOON
Prices subject to change without notice

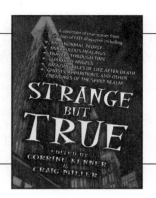

The Comet of Nostradamus
August 2004—Impact!

R.W. Welch

He foresaw the French Revolution and the rise of Napoleon. He perceived World War II 400 years before it happened as well as more recent events, such as the Persian Gulf War and the Reagan and Clinton administrations.

In this book, you will discover what Nostradamus saw for the years following 2000—a giant comet hurling toward Europe, and a great war extending throughout the Mediterranean and beyond.

What's more, scores of previously undeciphered or misapplied quatrains are successfully decoded, making *The Comet of Nostradamus* the most significant advance in Nostradamian interpretation since the work of Le Pelletier in the mid-nineteenth century.

Because the weight we give to Nostradamus' predictions for our times hinges on his accuracy in the past, a large portion of the book analyzes the percentage of Nostradmus' prophecies that qualify as psychic hits.

1-56718-816-8, 336 pp., 6 x 9   **$14.95**

To order call 1-800-THE MOON

Grave's End
A True Ghost Story

Elaine Mercado
Foreword by Hans Holzer

When Elaine Mercado and her first husband bought their home in Brooklyn, N.Y., in 1982, they had no idea that they and their two young daughters were embarking on a 13-year nightmare.

Within a few days of moving in, Elaine began to have the sensation of being watched. Soon her oldest daughter Karin felt it too, and they began hearing scratching noises and noticing weird smells. After they remodeled the basement into Karin's bedroom, the strange happenings increased, especially after Karin and her friends explored the crawl space under the house. Before long, they were seeing shadowy figures scurry along the baseboards and small balls of light bounce along the ceilings. Then the "suffocating dreams" started. Yet her husband refused to sell the house.

This book is the true story of how one family tried to adjust to living in a haunted house. It also tells how, with the help of parapsychologist Dr. Hans Holzer and medium Marisa Anderson, they discovered the identity of the ghosts and were able to assist them to the "light."

0-7387-0003-7, 192 pp., 6 x 9 $12.95

To order call 1-800-THE MOON
Prices subject to change without notice